february 2nd 2000

Santa Fe Tarot

Santa Fe Tarot

Holly Huber and Tracy LeCocq

Publisher

U.S. GAMES SYSTEMS, INC.
Stamford, CT 06902 USA

Library of Congress Number: 95-070427

ISBN: 0-88079-756-8

10 9 8 7 6 5 4 3 2 1

Printed in USA

U.S. Games Systems, Inc.
179 Ludlow Street
Stamford, CT 06902 USA

Contents

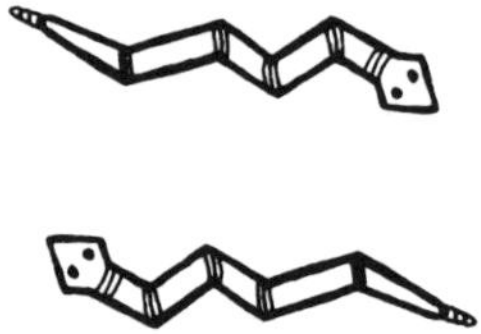

1

The Emergence Story

The beginning of the world, I am thinking about it.
The beginning of the world, I am talking about it.
Navajo

An old man, with long, unbound white hair, kneels on the dirt floor of a hogan. The dawn light filters over his shoulder and dances across the colored sand he is carefully painting onto a large circle on the floor. As he works the magic, he tells this story:

> Once, a very long time ago, the world was a dark and terrible place. It was called Black World or The Place of Running Pitch. Not many people lived there, and those who did were unhappy and sad. They wanted to leave, but were young and didn't know how to get out. Then Dragonfly made himself a pair of doubled wings and flew up into the black dome of the sky. Locust copied him and did the same. Soon, all beetles, flies, bees and even ants had tied wings to their backs and were flying into the dark, dark sky. Clever Locust spied a crack of blue light in the black ceiling and, though it was very difficult, they soon had all squeezed through into The Second World.

This was a blue, dimly-lit world, but The People were happy and content. Grass grew upon the ground and shrubs fleshed the earth. They would have spread out immediately, but Crane flew in from the east, Heron from the south, Grebe from the west, and Black-and-White Loon from the north. These big birds demanded that the small insect people leave, and return to their home at once. When the insect people explained their home was soon to be no more, Crane told them that there wasn't enough food in this place. The ants said they could live on grass seed; the locust on green leaves; the bees and flies claimed the honey from the blossoms; and the dragonflies said they could live on the pollen. When the big birds understood that these new small people wouldn't deprive them of their food, they agreed to allow them to stay, but demanded they not come near their homes. For a long time after that, the insect people lived in peace and harmony. One day they discovered that they had multiplied so greatly that they were having trouble finding food. All the leaves had been eaten and the pollen had blown away. The small people were hungry and unhappy again. They said, "Let us go to a new place."

Their moving created a great dust on the land, and huge clouds of dirt rose into the air as they winged their way to the place of the great birds. When the birds saw these terrible clouds, they declared war on the insects. The birds were much more powerful than the insects, and soon Locust declared, "We must leave this place, we must find a new place where the great birds do not rule."

Once again, the small people rose into the air and flew higher and higher. Finally they reached the hard blue dome of the sky and there heard a voice calling "This way, this way!" It was the voice of Blue Wind. He had created a spiral passage between the worlds and his voice led the fleeing insects through. But as they emerged, several birds followed them. (It is said this is why birds attack and make war on the insects even today.)

The Third World, or Yellow World, was much larger and brighter than the Blue World. In all four directions were high mountains. Rivers ran in three directions and many bright pools of water beckoned the small, beleaguered insects. They made friends with the first inhabitants and for a long while peace existed between them. Over the course of time, it became possible to distinguish the humans from the lower animals, the birds from the insects. Their language was all the same and they all had wings of some kind, but the humans wore theirs attached to fur or feather coats. They hadn't learned how to build houses yet, so they lived in caves and burrows. As they increased in number, they became crowded and unhappy. So, too, were the other animals, insects, and birds. They held a great meeting of all The People in the Third World. Lion, Wolf, Hummingbird, and Bluebird were named as strong, cunning, swift, and kind. They were sent to the edges of the world to bring back something useful to all The People. The one bringing back the most useful thing would be named Headman. The four travelers each brought a season and a time of day, and all were called Headman, which is why The People have never had a single chieftain, but rely upon a council of judges to this day.

There came a time when The People became restless in the Third World. The days and nights passed in endless yellow fog. The four travelers had not stayed with their donors long enough to learn how to use the gifts they brought The People and didn't know how to make morning or evening, light or darkness, winter or autumn. The four judges decided something must be done and called another huge clan meeting.

Again all The People decided to move and donned their wings and took to the sky. They were growing very tired, and many were on the verge of giving up when they heard a voice calling, "This way! Come this way!" Then they heard another voice, and yet another. From all points, all directions, they heard these eager voices. First Woman in the east, First Girl in the south, First Man in the west, and First Boy in the north all hid behind masks and called them to come with them to a place so beautiful and lovely, the Third World people were in awe.

The first Din'neh flew to the east and followed First Woman who taught them many things about their new world. The Bird People heeded the call of First Girl and flew to the south, which is why so many birds still fly south to escape the cold months of winter. The Animal People went to the west, where laws regarding hunting were formed, and the insects and crawlers flew to the north where it was so cold that most of them burrowed down or formed cocoons to keep them safe from the harsh winter.

This land was called The Black-and-White World, a place of darkness and daylight, of harsh and sharp contrasts. There were also many pitfalls. The worst one came about because of Coyote, whose trickery was notorious. Coyote was gambling with Water Monster one day. No matter how many times the stones and dice were changed, Coyote continued to win. Finally, Water Monster had nothing left to bet but his fine fur coat. And this too, he lost. When Coyote returned home, he hung Water Monster's fine coat on a peg, and only then discovered that Water Monster's tiny Water Babies were snugly wrapped in the sleeve of the coat. Since they were quiet and still, Coyote decided to say nothing and keep them.

Water Monster, however, upon learning that his babies had been stolen, flew into a terrible rage and shouted that he would destroy all The People and the land they lived upon. He opened all the flood gates in the oceans, releasing the water he knew was stored in the great caverns beneath the earth. The water rose higher and higher over the land. And finally, the people were forced to poke their heads through the turquoise dome in the center of the sky. But what they saw there, the beautiful rivers, the tall mountains, the lush green grasses, the rich red earth, convinced them to stay in this new world. This became known as the Fifth World, or the Emergence Place.

This is the story of how The Din'neh—The People—came to live in this world, and how from the day they arrived here the Holy Ones sent many gods to teach them the sacred knowledge that would forever lead the Din'neh on the Path of Beauty and Harmony.

Now that the Emergence story has been told, the healing ceremony can begin. The old man calls in the patient, and singing songs, administering herbs, and drawing the illness from the patient with the magic inherent in the story of the sandpainting, the medicine man leads the patient back into balance.

May it be beautiful before me.
May it be beautiful behind me.
May it be beautiful below me.
May it be beautiful above me.
May it be beautiful all around me.
In beauty it is finished.
NAVAJO

The Sandpainting

When The People first arrived in the Fifth World, they were ignorant of the ways of their new home. The old ones tell how The Pueblos, living on the far banks of the river, showed The People the ways to plant corn, and how to tend it, but The People knew little else. One day they heard voices calling to them, and when they looked, they saw four Yeis approaching, one from each of the four directions. The Yeis told them they had been sent to The People by the Holy Ones to teach them the ways to follow the Path of Beauty.

The Yeis told the Din'neh that the Universe was a very delicately balanced thing, full of enormously powerful forces that could release either good or evil. The Din'neh soon understood that if the balance was upset, even though by no intention of their own, some disaster would occur. This disaster usually resulted in illness.

In order to restore the balance, the Yeis told them, The People needed to perform one of the many Navajo Chants or Ways. These Chants or Ways are long and complex ceremonies that can last anywhere from one to nine days. They involve the use of songs, prayers, medicinal herbs, smoke, prayers, and sandpaintings.

A medicine man, or ha'atathli, skilled in a particular Way will arrive at the home of a person made ill by some upset in the balance of the Universe. Inside the hogan of the 'ill' person, he or she will prepare the sacred sandpainting. Each sandpainting reflects a part of the story needed to be told or sung that day to summon the necessary forces of that particular Way. The sandpainting is created in a careful and sacred manner, employing ancient knowledge of the art, and of the figures represented, and each design is completed in a specific order and executed using the five sacred colors: ocher, red, black, blue, and white. Other colors, such as brown, mauve, green, or orange are all considered variations of the sacred colors.

At the time of the sandpainting's creation, the entrance or opening of the sandpainting always faces East, as it is believed that evil can't as easily enter from that direction. The other three sides are protected, and this is usually accomplished by means of a Rainbow Guardian, a Yei whose figure borders the painting. Additional guardians are placed in the Eastern entrance point. (All paintings in The Santa Fe Tarot Deck should be considered, in their upright form, as facing East.)

The patient is then brought in and seated upon the completed sandpainting. Carefully, the medicine man touches first the sandpainting then the afflicted part of the patient. He is thus transferring the medicine and the power created in the sandpainting to the patient. When this process is complete, the sickness has fallen from the patient and harmony is restored.

The sandpainting is erased with a sacred feather staff before the sun sets that night. It is swept onto a blanket, carried outside and disposed of. By getting rid of it, the last of the sickness is literally carried away from the patient.

The Yeis, giving The People the Holy Ones' instructions, told them to do the sandpaintings directly on the surface of Mother Earth to prevent their knowledge from being hoarded, and to make certain that anyone with the necessary ability and patience might learn their intricate secrets.

The sandpaintings might have remained secret and forever to be created at sunrise only to disappear before sunset had it not been for a Navajo woman in the late 1890s who brought in a rug to a trading post near Shiprock, New Mexico.

The trader said he'd never seen anything like it and displayed it in his post. It had the figure of Yei-bih-chai dancer woven in it. Word of the amazing rug traveled swiftly and soon a censorious group of Navajo and at least one ha'atathli—medicine man—had arrived at the trading post to see the rug. They told the trader in no uncertain terms to remove the offensive rug from sight immediately. The trader did so, but sold the rug to an Eastern collector for a tremendous amount of money.

This was probably the single most significant sale of Native American art, for it changed the course of economic development and brought into permanence the mystical sandpainting. The sum of money paid for that one rug soon tempted others into creating other 'ceremonial' rugs. Even one ha'atathli, Hosteen Klah, most famous for his Hailway Chant (extinct since his death), wove many rugs with nearly complete sandpainting designs. It is said he did so in an effort to record some of the rapidly disappearing ceremonial knowledge.

Despite worldwide eagerness to see the sandpaintings, most ha'atathli still disapprove of the reproduction of sandpaintings, though they no longer actively fight to keep them from the public.

By 1947, a Navajo-produced sandpainting kit, complete with colored sand, was available on the market. Even some of the Navajo medicine apprentices used this kit to produce their first sandpaintings.

Early sandpaintings, and ceremonial sandpaintings today, were and are created with crushed sand or rocks of the desired colors. Sandstone, for example, when crushed, produces a rich rust-red color. Gypsum, when pulverized, produces a snowy white powder. The sand is shifted through the fingertips to achieve the desired pattern.

In The Santa Fe Tarot Deck, Holly Huber created her images by means of airbrushing with Dr. Martin Dyes, then carefully inking the painted figures and symbols.

Nowadays, it is a generally accepted practice to alter the sandpainting in some discreet manner when reproducing it for commercial use. The paintings can be altered in a number of ways: slight color variation from the traditional teachings, a crooked lightning instead of straight, inverted clouds rather than upright. Many people believe that by altering the sandpainting's traditional ceremonial perfection, the gods will not be angered, evil will not be encouraged, and the powerful forces that rule the Universe will not be upset.

In The Santa Fe Tarot Deck, each sandpainting has been modified and changed to preserve the integrity of the Navajo religious significance, and yet presented in as near a likeness as possible to offer the reader/diviner an opportunity to explore the rich symbology and the unique traditional art form given by the gods so that mankind could follow the Path of Beauty.

The Tarot

The art of divining the future or past by means of reading cards has its roots shrouded in mystery. Scholars differ on the origins of the Tarot, some claiming the symbolic cards were first developed in ancient China, while others hail its inception in ancient Egypt.

It is known, however, that the Tarot is closely related to many of the metaphysical aspects outlined in the mysterious Kabalah known to the ancient Hebrews, the mysteries of the Masonic Order still considered secret to this day, and the lore of Egyptian priesthood.

The earliest date attributed to the equivalent of present-day Tarot cards is the mid-15th century, and can be seen in decks of cards in European museums. In the Museo Correr in Venice, a deck of cards dates back to 1445, while another, called the Minchiati Deck, is said to be in a private collection in Milan.

Even in those early decks, there were two distinctly different components to the cards. The decks included a Major Arcana (*arcana* being the Latin word for secrets) consisting of 22 apocryphal cards dealing with mankind's spiritual journey, and the hopes, fears, joys, and sorrows encountered during that experience. The decks also contained the Minor Arcana, 56 cards consisting of four different suits, each of which contained four Court cards and ten numbered cards. The Minor Arcana is the forerunner of our modern-day playing cards, with the Page eliminated from the suits, leaving them with the mystical number of 13 cards per suit.

Whatever the source, whichever the origin, most scholars, mystics, and diviners agree that the Tarot speaks the language of symbology; perhaps, as Carl Jung suggested, a language that 'springs from the collective consciousness,' or the archetypal mind.

2

Symbology

When combining two such unique art forms as the tarot and Navajo sandpaintings, it would be natural to assume that something could get lost in the symbiosis. In the case of this marriage, however, the symbology is almost exactly correlative. Each concept inherent in the tarot is matched perfectly with a symbol or concept integral to Navajo myth.

For example, if the idea of beauty is called for by a particular tarot card, Navajo myth can offer Big Butterfly, who represents beauty. If healing is to be interpreted on a specific card, the Navajo medicine pouch is available.

Even the five sacred colors correspond directly to tarot concepts. Ocher or yellow indicates some degree of strife, where blue or green shows a harmonious connection. Black and white are neither good or bad by themselves, but are tremendously powerful colors that show strength and spirit. Red often corresponds to emotion, catastrophe, or fierce protection. The Navajo religion and its epic myths are presented in ceremonial Ways by directly recreating a specific account of a heroic incident involving the gods. When recounting the Emergence Story during a 'sing,' therefore, the actual characters that centrally appear in the story are painted upon the sand.

Nearly every one of these epic characters relates directly to one of the Major Arcana cards in the tarot or to one of the four Court cards in the four Minor Arcana suits. While the accompanying myths with each card reveal some of the symbology presented, the complex imagery and symbology common among Navajo Ways will be new to many, and therefore could be difficult to follow. The significance of the individual symbols is outlined below to aid the reader/diviner in interpreting the meaning of The Santa Fe Tarot Deck.

The Navajo used in this book has been anglicised & phoenetically altered, I have written it in authentic navajo.

Symbol Interpretation

Arrow Often a guardian, showing fierce protection. Sometimes in hand, indicating strength, power or strife.

Bent Figures When skirts and legs are at an angle, it indicates strife.

Cloud Clouds bring rain, and rain brings growth, life. A good sign; good luck.

Cloud Rattles Shows the power to bring Rain Gods or Rainbow People. A good sign; good luck.

Cloud Tower Upright clouds stacked upon one another indicate great blessings. Inverted, terrible storm brewing.

Cornbeetle A powerful Yei who brings much good to The People.

Earth Circle Can display the four directions, four seasons, four elements, four sacred plants. A sign of wealth, of good things.

Earrings Shows person has 'hard goods' or jewelry, indicates wealth, security in position.

Feathers A single feather shows a rather solitary standing; more feathers indicate wealth, stature, security.

Flint Used for warrior's clothing. Offers protection and readiness to fight.

Fly Big Fly, one of the first Yeis. Can carry many upon his back. Shows strength or wisdom.

Frog Big Frog can capture or rescue an innocent. Usually indicates weighed judgment.

Jugs Sacred water jugs can only be carried by very powerful Yeis or by Water Creatures or Water People. Confers grace, agility.

Knotted String A string with knots in it indicate something which has to be remembered, i.e., days or ceremonies.

Lightning Straight lightning is considered an arrow from the bow of one of the Thunders or from the Fire-god, and is usually a good omen. Crooked lightning is either an arrow or a fire serpent of the sky world and can be either good or bad, depending upon other images.

Logs Used to indicate fire, hearth. Usually appears in conjunction with a tipi or sacred plant.

Medicine Pouch Also called medicine bundle. Usually presented dangling from Yei's arm. Indicates healing powers, strength, wisdom. Can also show intuition, psychic knowledge.

Moon A deity created by Changing Woman, often serving as a guardian or protector. Usually paired with the Sun.

Otter An important personage in Navajo legend, Otter attempts peace or reconciliation. Can indicate a cessation to war.

Plants The four sacred plants: bean, squash, corn, and tobacco. Usually shown pointing to the four directions. Always beneficial.

Seeds Depicted as small black dots, seeds either in a skirt or elsewhere show the ability to make things grow, and indicate potential.

Spruce Often confused with feathers, the blue spruce branches confer wisdom and the ability to harmonize with nature.

Stars Occasionally the constellations are presented in the dress of one of the Yeis. These show power and far-reaching knowledge.

Tipi Used in traditional or stylized form to indicate a fondness for home. Sometimes used as a guardian.

Water Zigzag lines over each other simply announce the presence of water, one of life's most powerful natural forces.

Water Trails Not to be confused with curved rainbows, these irregular curved blue bands are trails to follow to water. Indicates guidance, safety.

Weasel Pouch A unique medicine bundle that only the very intuitive can use. Confers great healing power and the ability to dream.

Weasel Prong Similar in nature to weasel pouch. Used predominantly to indicate an affinity with nature, with things of the earth.

Zia Lines radiating out from a circle, usually equated with the Sun's rays stretching in all directions. A positive influence.

(Other symbols should be interpreted by intuition.)

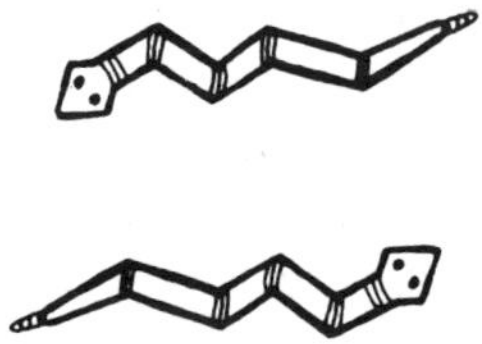

3

The Major Arcana

In a holy place with a god I walk,
In a holy place with a god I walk.
On a chief of mountains with a god I walk.
In old age wandering with a god I walk.
On a trail of beauty with a god I walk.
Navajo

The Major Arcana, consisting of 22 apocryphal cards, keyed from 0, The Fool (Rainboy), to XXI, The World (Emergence Place), is believed to illustrate the life of a human being, from joys and sorrows, to hopes and fears. Each of the Major Arcana cards represents a distinct principle, law or power in nature.

The initial creators of the Major Arcana—if indeed 'creators' is the correct concept—must have been at least acquainted with the Kabalah, the ancient Hebrew book of metaphysics, because the number of Major Arcana cards directly corresponds with the mystic numbers outlined in that book. The number of letters in the Hebrew alphabet is also 22, and many of the cards are said to suggest symbolic meanings synthesized from the Tree of Life, the central symbol in Kabalistic wisdom.

It should be noted that the Fool card, keyed with a 0, can be placed at either the beginning or end of the Major Arcana. The Fool card, therefore, can represent the self, the dreamer as one who would learn; or can indicate the end, the one moving to another plane, having learned the lessons of this life.

Each of the Major Arcana cards presented in The Santa Fe Tarot Deck is accompanied by the Navajo myth most closely relating to the concept inherent in the Tarot. The reader/diviner is advised to carefully read the myth to assimilate the Navajo legend before proceeding to the suggested interpretations.

O THE FOOL — Rainboy

Myth Once there was a boy called Rainboy who loved to play games, and in particular, he loved to gamble on the games. Unfortunately, Rainboy wasn't a very good player of games and was a worse gambler. He kept losing his games and his bets. When he had lost all his clothing, his silver belt, and his horse, his family tied him up and promised to whip him the next morning. During the night, a bat came in secrecy and used magic to help him escape. Alone and poor, Rainboy was forced to make his way in the world as best he could. One day, he accidentally angered Big Thunder, and as a result of White Thunder's rescuing him, a huge battle broke out between the Thunder Yeis. Rainboy, however, atoning for his misdeeds, intervened. A peace was made between the Thunders, and in gratitude, they taught Rainboy the very powerful healing ceremony, the Hailway Chant (now extinct). Rainboy figures into many of the chant ways of the Navajo. The central theme of the stories is always the same, however, depicting

Rainboy as the dreamer, the boy who falls into trouble through his carelessness and yet somehow manages to get out of trouble through his desire to achieve good.

Symbology Rainboy dances with snakes coming from his feet, showing he travels to many unusual places. He holds crooked lightning in one hand and a wand in the other to give him power and vision. From the wand hand dangle rattles which grant him joy and dreams. Guardian Bats protect him, having saved him once from his parents' wrath, and they flank a barred rainbow headdress with many small corn people showing Rainboy's ability to please and entertain, and yet, because the headdress does not actually touch Rainboy, his dreams may be distant. Rainboy is depicted here with a turquoise blue blouse and red skirt.

Suggested Interpretations The subject is a dreamer, a mystic. He or she has the desire to accomplish a great goal but must be careful to make the right choice. If he thinks that 'when ignorance is bliss, 'tis folly to be wise,' then he is indeed the fool.

Reversed Folly, indiscretion, thoughtless action. The choice made is likely to be faulty.

Guardians Twin Bats, indicating the magic that freed Rainboy from his bonds.

I THE MAGICIAN — Orangewind Yei

Myth It happened one day that the twin sons of The Sun were traveling and came to a place called White-Streak-of-the-Ashes. From there they went down the west side of the mountain and found people living there. The people were red in color and their hair was curly and hung down on their backs. One of them said to the Twins, "Where are you coming from? Earth surface people are not allowed here." He told them he was called Orangewind, and in return for their promise to leave, gave them a red stone and taught them the words of the Reckless Coyoteway, chants to teach them the wisdom of learning and remembering.

Symbology Orangewind wears a tremendous eagle or thunderbird headdress denoting his lofty aspirations and creative magic. His headdress is so large, offering so much protection, he doesn't require guardians. He relies on the magic he carries, crooked lightning in one hand, a bull-roarer in the other. Rattles dangle from both arms while a medicine stick and medicine pouch extend from his left hand. Feathers shoot from his feet, carrying him far and high.

Suggested Interpretations Will, mastery, organizational skills. Originality. Creativity. Imagination. Spontaneity. Self-confidence. Ingenuity. Flexibility. Masterfulness. Self-control. Sleight of hand. Ability to take the power from above and manifest it.

Reversed Weakness of will. Ineptitude. Insecurity. Disquiet. Delay. The use of one's skills or power for destructive ends.

Guardians None.

II THE HIGH PRIESTESS — Corn-Cloud Woman

Myth Also known as Changing Woman, Corn-Cloud Woman is said to have been born with the power of senescence and rejuvenation. The abducted children of Rock Crystal Talking God witnessed this transformation when they were taken to her home in the Western Ocean to be taught the Blessingway healing chant. She is also said to change four different ways, from White Shell Woman to Turquoise, Abalone or Jet Woman. First Man called her Changing Woman after she began transforming every four days. Others called her Changing Woman because they believed her four transformations represented the four seasons.

Symbology In her right hand, Corn-Cloud Woman carries a weasel pouch to indicate her wisdom and perception. In her left, she holds another medicine pouch, this one adorned with feathers, signifying intuition and far-reaching thought. She wears a feathered headdress as well, and the rainbow border surrounding her is also capped and underscored with feathers.

Suggested Interpretations Unrevealed future, hidden influences at work. Transformation. Wisdom. Sound judgment. Common sense. Serenity. Objectivity. Penetration. Foresight. Intuition. Perception. Self-reliance. Emotionlessness. Platonic relationships.

Reversed Conceit. Sensual enjoyment. Shortsightedness. Selfishness. Passion. Physical ardor. Acceptance of superficial knowledge. Bad judgment.

Guardians Butterflies, signifying beauty and wisdom, serve as Corn-Cloud Woman's guardians.

Changing Woman
Asdzą́ą́ Nádleehé

The grandmother of the Navajo
mother of the Hero Twins,
Monster Slayer = Naayéé' Neezghání
Born for Water – Tó Bájísh Chíní

III THE EMPRESS — Mother Earth

Myth Mother Earth, or Nahas-tsan behassun, appears in most of the Navajo Ways, including the Shootingway, Mountainway, and the Blessingway. It is said that the first creation of the Great Spirit was Father Sky and Mother Earth, from whence all life springs. Before Changing Woman, before First Woman, and before The People, Mother Earth took all the world to her bosom and made it grow, mature, bear fruit and, finally, return to her. She does this even now and is still the source from which springs the seed of all living things. She is eternally and permanently linked with her mate, Father Sky. One need only look at the horizon to see their joyous union.

Symbology Mother Earth wears a horned headdress and a rainbow mask. In her hands she carries the earth, divided into elements, and her body is filled with the four sacred plants, corn, tobacco, bean, and squash. Feathers lift her legs and adorn the rainbow border protecting her.

Suggested Interpretations Feminine progress. Fertility, fruitfulness. Accomplishment. Mother. Sister. Wife. Marriage. Children. Feminine influence. Ability to motivate others. Practicality. Intuition.

Reversed Vacillation. Inaction. Lack of interest. Lack of concentration. A frittering away of resources. Indecision. Delay. Anxiety. Infertility. Infidelity.

Guardians Mother Earth's guardian is the arrow, granting her the ability to protect others.

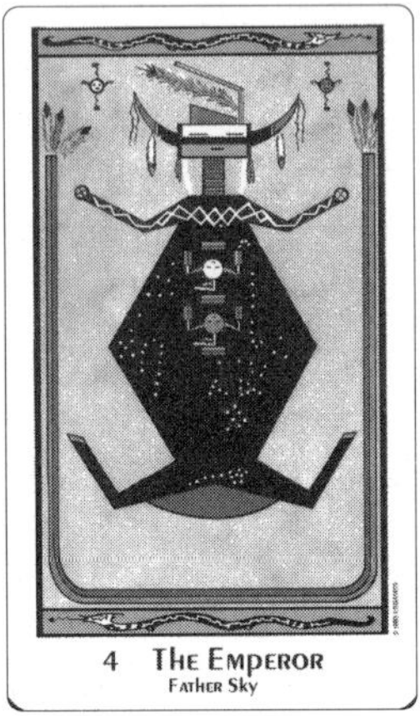

IV THE EMPEROR — Father Sky

Myth Father Sky, Yaah-dklith beh-hasteen—along with his mate, Mother Earth—was the first creation of the Great Spirit. Father Sky governs the stars, the moon, the sun, and the constellations that make up his body. Even the Milky Way, represented here by the zigzag white lines across his shoulders, is a part of Father Sky. He holds the world and its seasons in his hands, and they are painted yellow to show his domination and war-like nature. From his union with Mother Earth came the Holy Ones who taught The People the healing ways.

Symbology Father Sky is one of the few male Yeis to have the square head normally assigned to female deities. Like his mate, Mother Earth, Father Sky wears a horned headdress, but his mask is the yellow-and-black of the warrior. Inside him, the sun, moon, and stars are seen, depicting his influence over all he sees. Like his mate, his hands hold the earth and all its elements, and his rainbow border is adorned by the feathers of intuition, although his are colored with war colors.

Suggested Interpretations Leadership. Worldly power. Confidence. Wealth. Stability. Authority. Indomitable spirit. War-making tendencies. Father. Brother. Husband. Male influence. Domination of intelligence and reason over emotion and passion. Patriarchal figure. Controlled sexual drive.

Reversed Immaturity. Ineffectiveness. Indecision. Inability. Weakness of character. Failure to control petty emotions. Possible bondage to one's parents.

Guardians Sun and Moon guardians offer him protection both day and night.

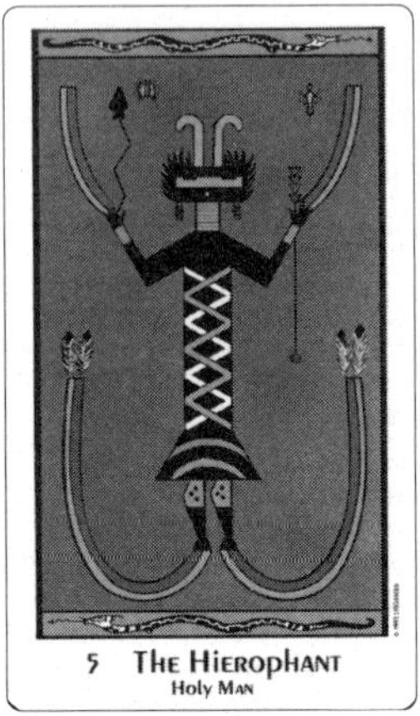

V THE HIEROPHANT — Holy Man

Myth As a powerful ha'atathli, Holy Man traveled far and wide to learn the powers of many different peoples until he, himself, became a Yei. One day Holy Man went hunting with his brother Holy Boy. He shot a Mountain Sheep with an arrow decorated with feathers he'd taken from a bird he'd stolen. Angered, the Thunder People used lightning bolts to capture him and took him to the Sky People to be punished. Luckily, Big Fly and Otter protected his skin from the lightning and helped persuade the Sky People to spare him. With the Sky People, Holy Man learned ceremonies to cure people who had illnesses created by lightning.

Symbology Holy Man wears a Mountain Sheep headdress, signifying his wisdom, and a feathered mask to show his adherence to old ways. Curved rainbows extend from his hands and feet, showing his powerful nature and his innate kindness. He carries a crooked spear in his left hand and a bull-roarer and medicine wand in his right. His dress is dark and warrior-like, with jagged lightning as a reminder of his narrow escape, and giving him a somber, oppressive air.

Suggested Interpretations Ritualism. Mercy. Kindness. Forgiveness. Inspiration. Compassion. Servitude. Inactivity. Timidity. Captivity to one's own ideas. Tendency to cling to outmoded ideas and principles. Conformity. A religious or spiritual leader.

Reversed Foolish generosity. Susceptibility. Impotence. Vulnerability. Frailty. Unorthodox. Renunciation. Openness to new ideas.

Guardians A butterfly and an otter or frog serve as his guardians, lending him both beauty and cunning.

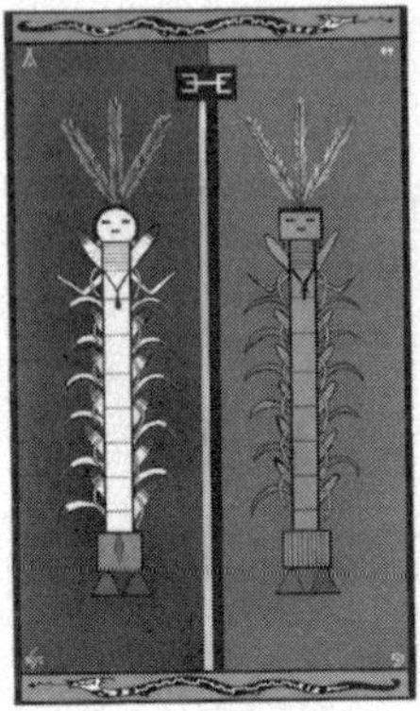

6 The Lovers
White Corn Man—Yellow Corn Woman

VI THE LOVERS — White Corn Man — Yellow Corn Woman

Myth One of the Follower Pairs, White Corn Man and Yellow Corn Woman, often are referred to as Two-who-follow-one-another, or in other versions (particularly in the Blessingway) as Long Life-Happiness. It is said that Changing Woman created the Corn People from jewel corn figures in a bundle First Man gave her. The first of these people were White Corn Man and Yellow Corn Woman, Grand Corn People, who each possess twelve full ears of corn upon their bodies. The mating of White Corn Man and Yellow Corn Woman resulted in the birth of Corn People. It is they who, with Changing Woman, and Talking and Calling Gods, taught The People the raising and caring of corn. The Mating of Corn ceremony is one of the fourth versions of a Blessingway rite.

Symbology White Corn Man and Yellow Corn Woman seem eternally apart here, and yet are forever linked by

Corn-Beetle who interrupts the separation. Depicted here in their Yei form, both have many ears of ripe corn waiting to be plucked and both have large feather headdresses showing their idealism and faith.

Suggested Interpretations Choice. Temptation. Strong attraction. Love. Beauty. Perfection. Harmony. Trust. Beginning of a romance. Deep feeling. Optimism. Freedom of emotion. The necessity of testing or of subjecting to trial. Struggle between sacred and profane love. A meaningful affair.

Reversed Failure to meet the test. Unreliability. Separation. Frustration in love and marriage. Interference. Fickleness. Unwise plans.

Guardians In lieu of formal guardians, White Corn Man and Yellow Corn Woman are protected by the four-corner placement of the tipi, clouds, fish, and hearth, representing the four elements.

VII THE CHARIOT — B'Ganaskiddy

Myth Known in English by a variety of names—Hump-backed Yei, Navajo God of Plenty or of Harvest, and Camel God—B'Ganaskiddy travels the world with his deerskin back-pack of seeds. He gives the seeds to The People for planting, and upon harvest, returns to gather some of the seeds for safekeeping. In this way, The People will never go hungry, for B'Ganaskiddy continually roams and carries with him the seeds needed for the future.

Symbology The seeds B'Ganaskiddy carries can be clearly seen housed in his blue back-pack. In this version, he wears the traditional Mountain Sheep horned-headdress, decorated with black and white feathers. He holds a medicine pouch and a double bull-roarer in his hands indicating his strength and wisdom. The mountains beneath his feet show the distances he must travel in his journeys. His red blouse contains white jagged lightning, as does his blue skirt. His skirt is also fringed and jeweled.

Guiding his travels is a short rainbow bar that hangs in the sky beneath his hands.

Suggested Interpretations Triumph, success. Control over the forces of nature—thus triumph over difficulties of both health and enemies. Adversity, possibly already overcome. Conflicting influences. Turmoil. Vengeance. Success. Possibly a voyage or journey. Escape. Rushing into a decision. Need to pay attention to details. Urgency to gain control of one's emotions.

Reversed Failure. To lose at the last minute something otherwise in your grasp. Sudden collapse of plans. Overwhelmed. Failure to face reality. Desire for change without careful consideration.

Guardians None.

Ghą́ą́'ask'idii

The Humpback yei'ii

The "hump" being a deerskin bag full of seeds.

is this men, also Kokopelli?

VIII STRENGTH — Monster Slayer

Myth Known as Nayenezgani, and also The-Slayer-of-Alien-Gods, Monster Slayer is one of the Twin Warrior Gods, sons of The Sun. Monster Slayer comes to protect The People from catastrophes such as earthquakes, hurricanes, cyclones, and wars—anything that is not in the Path of Beauty and Harmony. Monster Slayer and his brother, First Born or Born of Water (Tobaschischin) are responsible for destroying most of the terrible monsters, or Yei-tso, who roamed the earth in its early days. Monster Slayer is called upon today by a ha'atathli to put an end to the calamities befalling man, because the Navajo know that man, in his ignorance, may produce such disasters. One of the few Yei-tso not destroyable by Monster Slayer is Death.

Symbology Monster Slayer is armed with crooked lightning, given to him by his father, the Sun. His dress is decorated with wide bands of crooked lightning, and crooked lightning crosses him, pointing in all directions.

He stands upon a double-headed lightning bolt. Indicating that he is on the warpath, he is surrounded by black, and a large red crooked lightning decorates him.

Suggested Interpretations Force of character. Spiritual power overcoming material power. Strength. Courage. Conviction. Energy. Defiance. Action. Confidence. Zeal. Matter over mind or mind over matter. Accomplishment.

Reversed Domination of the material. Weakness. Pettiness. Impotence. Sickness. Lack of faith. Abuse of power. Succumbing to temptation. Indifference.

Guardians His guardians are twin Suns.

→ To'Bájísh Chíní

9 The Hermit
Pollen Boy on the Sun

IX THE HERMIT — Pollen Boy on the Sun

Myth Pollen Boy, one of the Holy People, is a central figure in the Creation Story. It is said that he takes his place on The Sun so that The Sun might not be as lonely and take a rest, thus allowing The People and their plants and animals an escape from the burning heat of The Sun. He is also one, along with Cornbeetle Girl, appointed to provide guidance for the Talking Gods. Pollen Boy, called Trahdah-de'en-eshki, appears on The Sun in the Blessingway and is used for either boy or hunter. Without the sacred plants, traditionally the painting would be used for a man.

Symbology Depicted here as a single blue character, Pollen Boy stands upon the Sun's mouth, flanked by two short rainbow bars and his hands seemingly cupping The Sun's eyes. The Sun is huge and shown here with red and black eagle feathers, and black, lightning-decorated horns.

Suggested Interpretations Silent counsel. Knowledge. Solicitude. Prudence. Receiving wisdom from above. Discretion. Vigilance. Circumspection. Self-denial. Withdrawal. Regression. Annulment. Tendency to withhold emotion. Possible meeting with someone who might guide the seeker on a path to spiritual discovery.

Reversed Imprudence. Hastiness. Rashness. Immaturity. Incorrect advice. Failure caused by dullness. Rejection of growth or change.

Guardians None.

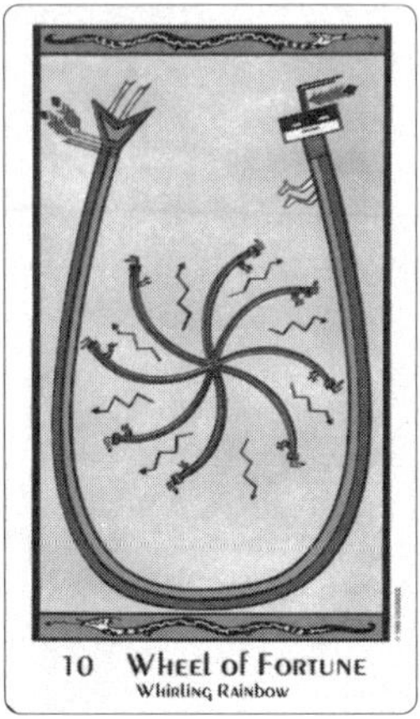

X WHEEL OF FORTUNE — Whirling Rainbow

Myth The Rainbow Guardian's mission and message are usually moisture in the air, abundance on the earth, new growth and new life coming through the color of the rainbow. These are said to reflect the heart center of all seeds and the quickening that will soon come to pass. The clockwise movement of the Whirling Rainbow Yeis reflects the rotation of the earth, the balance between night and day, and gentle balance of the seasons. The crooked lightning between each of the Whirling Rainbow Yeis point to all directions of the earth. They are one of the most powerful forces of the Creative Spirit and are often seen by those who walk the Path of Beauty.

Symbology A single, right-sided Rainbow Yei with black and white face and blue feathers borders eight Whirling Rainbow Yeis all connected and spinning clockwise. Crooked lightning of different lengths and heights float in between each Whirling Yei, pointing in all directions, and yet, all are just out of grasp.

Suggested Interpretations Success. Destiny. Fortune. Fate. Outcome. Culmination. Approaching the end of a problem. Good or bad luck, depending on influences of nearby cards. Inevitability. The wheel suggests the course of events from beginning to end. Advancement for better or worse. Creative evolution.

Reversed Failure of an enterprise. Bad luck. Broken sequence. Interruption or inconsistency due to unexpected events. Outside influence not contemplated. The reaping of what has been sown.

Guardians None.

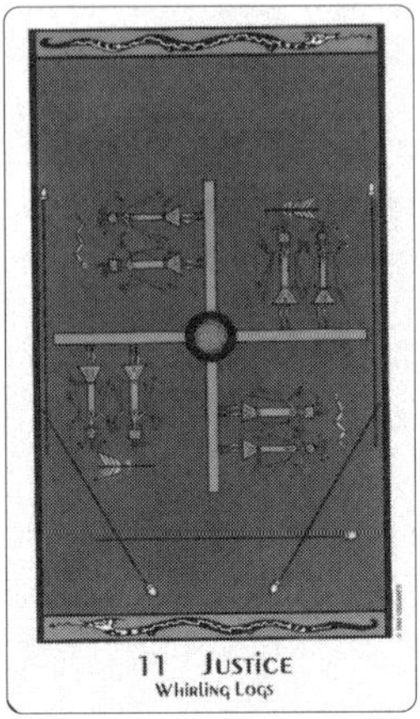

XI JUSTICE — Whirling Logs

Myth Variations of the Whirling or Floating Logs sandpainting occur in the Plumeway and Waterway chants, but Whirling Logs are known best for their inclusion in the Nightway Chant. This sandpainting is usually created on the Sixth Night of the Nightway, during the Visionary portion of the chant. In this story, a man sits thinking that he needs longer and stronger songs. Talking God appeared to him and told him he knew where he could go to get more songs. The man followed him to a mystical place where eight Yeis riding upon their Whirling Logs provided the additional healing information.

Symbology Two Yeis, male and female, stand upon each of the four logs radiating out from a circle that represents the earth. Two sets of the Yeis are topped with a crooked snake showing the inclination for advancement and travel, and the other two are capped with arrows showing their readiness to fight for their rights. All carry many rattles and feathers indicating their flexibility and wisdom. The Whirling Logs sandpainting depicted here is bordered by crossed spears.

Suggested Interpretations May bespeak desire for education. Reasonableness. Justice. Proper balance. Harmony. Equity. Righteousness. Virtue. Honor. Virginity. Just reward. The eventual outcome, whether favorable or unfavorable, will be truly fair to the person concerned. Equilibrium. Poise. Impartiality.

Reversed Bias. False accusations. Bigotry. Severity in judgment. Legal action taken. Intolerance. Unfairness. Abuse.

Guardians None.

XII THE HANGED MAN — Blue Whirlwind Boy

Myth Blue Whirlwind Boy figures into many of the Navajo Windways and in the Chiricahua Windway as well. He is the son of Dark or Black Wind and, while individual versions vary, the basic story is referred to as the Killing of Whirlwind Boy and is found in The Journey for Knowledge and Power. Blue Whirlwind Boy was rash, ignoring his father's command to stay at the hogan. He was kidnapped by first the Thunders, then by the Cyclone People. Dark Wind was very worried and feared his son was dead. Blue Whirlwind Boy was very frightened and managed to escape to hide in a hole in the rocks. Dark Wind begs for the boy's life and it is restored by the supernaturals in the Restoration By Stepping Over and Marking Away ceremony.

Symbology Blue Whirlwind Boy is depicted here as a trapped figure, his whirlwind rattles in warrior colors, his crooked lightning spilling from his hands. Trapped suns serve as his rattles and hang above his head, as though behind him, and signify his time in hiding. An unarmed, non-headdressed Rainbow Yei with a warrior's colored mask serves as his border.

Suggested Interpretations Life in suspension. Transition. Change. Reversal of the mind and in one's way of life. Apathy and dullness. Abandonment. Renunciation. The change of life's forces. The period of respite between significant events. Sacrifice. Repentance. Readjustment. Regeneration. The approach of new life forces.

Reversed Lack of sacrifice. Unwillingness to make the necessary effort. Failure to give of oneself. Egotism. False prophecy. Useless sacrifice.

Guardians Snake guardians, which would ordinarily flank his head, run from his feet instead.

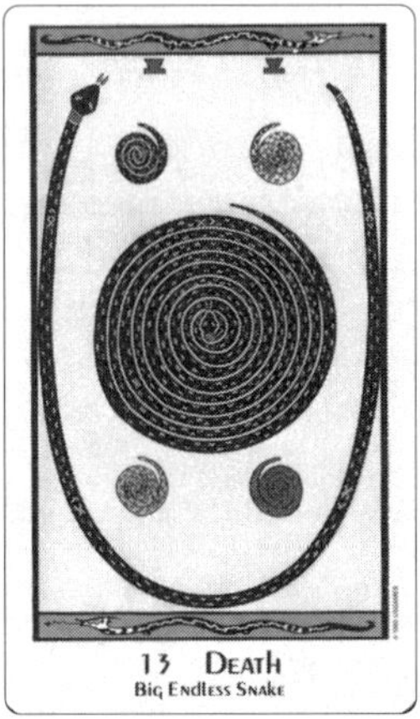

XIII DEATH — Big Endless Snake

Myth Big Endless Snake appears in many of the sandpainting ceremonies, including the Beautyway, Big Starway, Windway and Shootingway. In one tale, the hero uses poisonous tobacco to overcome Big Endless Snake and render him unconscious. Big Snake's wife pleads with the hero to restore her husband, in exchange for all their goods, both soft and hard. The hero restores Big Endless Snake and learns the sandpaintings and ceremonial knowledge he really had sought in the first place. Big Endless Snake is a mythological being, sometimes considered evil and dangerous. All snakes' tongues are red (danger) and are said to have the power of reducing Cyclone to Whirlwinds. Each time a Big Endless Snake is used in a Way, the result sought is that of transformation, which is appropriate for he represents eternal change with no beginnings, no endings.

Symbology Big Endless Snake curls in the center of the card, as though ready to strike—or to transform. It is accompanied by four smaller Endless Snakes, black and yellow on the left, white and green on the right. A large guardian snake borders the painting, and is marked with deer tracks.

Suggested Interpretations Transformation. Clearing away the old to make way for the new. Unexpected change. Loss. Alteration. Abrupt change of the old self through not necessarily physical death. The end of a familiar situation or friendship. Financial loss. A new era. Illness, possibly death. Birth of new ideas.

Reversed Stagnation. Immobility. Slow changes. Partial change. Inertia. Narrowly avoiding a serious accident. Revolution, political upheaval.

Guardians Two cloud guardians highlight the way to the future.

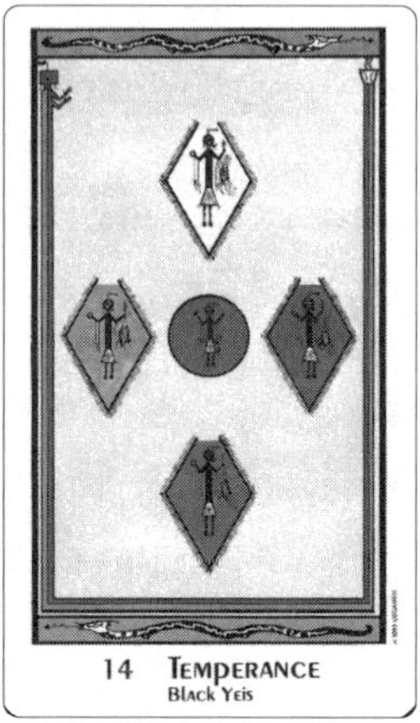

XIV TEMPERANCE — Black Yeis

Myth The Black Gods or Yeis appear most notably in variations of the Nightway Chant and are used in sandpaintings begun on the ninth day of the ceremony and removed that night after the sun sets. The Black Yeis, called Hash-Jaish-Jinnh, are summoned from their home at The Black Ground, though often must be sought in the stars. It is sometimes difficult to find them, but usually they appear at the eleventh hour, raggedy and nearly clownish. The other Gods stop the people from laughing when they arrive at the hogan of a person. They are always called upon during the final day of the healing ceremony as the Black Yeis are themselves ha'atathli or strong medicine men, and they bring with them the power to heal or restore harmony to the ailing patient. It is the Black Yeis who bring the cornmeal and cakes which will be consumed at the conclusion of the ceremony.

Symbology Inside a Rainbow Yei border, four Black Yeis in diamond-shaped, fringed medicine pouches hover on all points of the compass. Each carries the earth in one hand, a feather and an elaborately decorated medicine Rattle hang from both arms. Sacred plants adorn each skirt. The four Black Yeis appear to restore harmony to the central figure. The central figure carries a bull-roarer in one hand and the other is open-palmed, accepting the Black Yeis' assistance.

Suggested Interpretations Adaptation, tempering, coordination. Moderation. Temperance. Patience. Accomplishment through self-control and frugality. Accommodation. Harmony. The mixing or bringing together into perfect union. Management. Fusion. Adjustment. Good influence. Consolidation.

Reversed Discord. Conflict of interest. Hostility. Inability to work with others. Difficulty in understanding others. Impatience. Sterility. Separation.

Guardians None.

XV THE DEVIL — Sand Dune Monster

Myth The Sand Dune Monster is one of the many monsters that Monster Slayer and Born-of-Water (First Born) were sent to battle, but he is one that recurs often in the lives of The People. He lurks in the desert, lying in wait for those wishing to cross the desert mountains. He sets traps for The People, capturing them by trickery and deception. He attempts to lead them from the Path of Beauty and Harmony and then, once having taken them, tries to hold them captive permanently. Sand Dune Monster appears in a ceremony called The Two Who Went to Their Father, and figures in episodes of the Enemyway Chant.

Symbology Wearing red with a double-headed crooked lightning shirt, Sand Dune Monster also wears a cross-horned mask with jagged feathers, painted yellow for war. He is open-palmed, his feet are square and both palms and soles of his feet contain small yellow-white circles, signifying his attempt to hold the world. Trapped in the sandy mountains are Corn-Cloud Yei, Many-Cloud-People Yei, Cactus Yei, and Many-Cactus-People Yei. Over the mountains is a tri-colored rainbow, and having traveled it are the Twin War Gods who are there to battle Sand Dune Monster.

Suggested Interpretations Ravage. Bondage. Malevolence. Subservience. Downfall. Weird experience. Bad outside influence or advice. Black magic. Unexpected failure. Inability to realize goals. Violence. Shock. Fatality. Self-punishment. Temptation to evil. Self-destruction.

Reversed The beginning of spiritual understanding. Release from bondage. Throwing off shackles. Divorce. Recognition of one's needs by another person. Overcoming severe handicaps. The overcoming of pride and self-interest.

Guardians None, although the Twin War Gods serve as a warning to Sand Dune Monster.

XVI THE TOWER — Red Thunder Yei

Myth One of the Thunders, this Red Thunder Yei is depicted headless, and is therefore terrifying. The Thunders are notorious for capturing people, although most return those hapless folk without horrible damage. Red Thunder Yei is a figure no longer appearing in traditional sandpaintings, as the knowledge of him has crossed into myth and the chant he appeared in is now extinct. The painting here is drawn from descriptive tales and legends which tell of the terrible red and yellow lightning that shoot from his angry fingers and the multitude of Yeis captured and held in his many-tiered wings. Speared lightning streaks upward from his headless neck, crossing four blood-red feathers, indicating his wrath.

Symbology Warlike yellow and red crooked lightning without points fork from yellow-tipped open hands with small black circles showing the world already taken. Red and yellow crooked lightning shoots from each tier of the Red Thunder Yei's wings as well, showing his wrath and power. Two male and female Yeis peer fearfully from each level on each side of the wings as they are about to be spilled out. Fanged snakes approach each foot instead of drawing away from them, showing his self-absorption and the need for transformation.

Suggested Interpretations Complete and sudden change. Breakdown of old beliefs. Abandonment of past relationships. Severing of a friendship. Changing one's opinion. Unexpected events. Bankruptcy. Downfall. Loss of stability. Loss of security. Overthrow of existing ways of life.

Reversed Continued oppression. Following old ways. Living in a rut. Inability to effect any worthwhile change. Entrapment in an unhappy situation. Could indicate the gain of freedom of body or mind at great cost.

Guardians None.

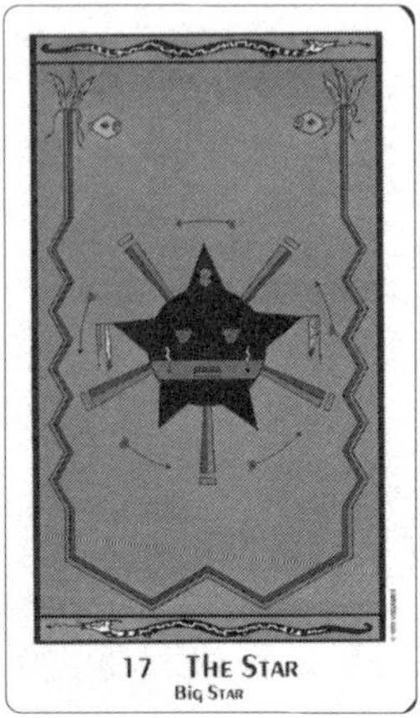

XVII THE STAR — Big Star

Myth Big Star, who figures in many Navajo stories and chants, apparently only appears in one sandpainting done in the Navajo Windway ceremonial healing. The only reproduction of Big Star is a pencil sketch drawn, many believe, by the great singer, Lefthanded, who told of a third ceremonial sandpainting of a large star surrounded by five arrows. In his story, Four Big Star People, feeling the need of the regular singer, came from far away to sing in place of the ha'atathli. Upon discovering a 'bad person'—Small Owl—among the spectators, they motioned with arrows and killed it, thus freeing the ailing person of bad influences. Big Star is also mentioned frequently, but depicted differently, in the Big Starway chant.

Symbology Big Star is stationary in the sky, but counter-clockwise movement is shown by the arrows between his rainbow rays. He wears a feather-and-bead headdress hanging in perfect balance from the widest two points of his five-pointed face, and he has black-and-white crooked lightning aiming downward into his faceband. Twin suns crown him while inverted clouds filled with sand make up his eyes, all of which denote his affinity with the elements.

Suggested Interpretations Hope. Faith. Inspiration. Bright prospects. Mixing of the past and present. Optimism. Insight. Astrological influence. Fulfillment. Pleasure. The proper balance of desire and work, hope and effort, love and expression. Unselfish aid.

Reversed Unfulfilled hopes. Disappointment. Pessimism. Bad luck. Lack of opportunity. Stubbornness. Bull-headed. Imbalance. Conclusion of an unsatisfactory business experience or social friendship.

Guardians Big Star's guardians are bats, showing his insight and inclination to provide assistance. He is protected by a crooked rainbow border with lofty feathers and beads.

Stars = Są'tsoh = North Star
= Náhookǫs - Big Dipper
= Nákǫǫkos little Dipper
= Są' Doo Nídízídí - Morning Star

XVIII THE MOON — The Moon

Myth When First Woman and First Man appeared in the present world, The People complained to them that they needed more differences in the seasons and in the light. After trying many ways, First Woman decided she must find a better way to light the earth. She fashioned two round wheels of equal-sized quartz. The People decorated the wheels and took them to the top of the Eastern Peak. But they complained to First Woman that the discs needed to move. Then two old wise men stepped forward and said they would give their spirits to The Sun and The Moon, thus giving the decorated wheels life and power to move across the sky. They were each given feathers to drop in regular intervals, and one was to wait until the other had dropped all the feathers before rising himself.

Symbology As The Moon is used in sandpaintings not to commemorate any specific event in a myth, but rather to evoke sacred powers, it usually appears in purest form, a pale replica of The Sun. The Moon wears two broad, striped horns with dangling feathers and beads indicating superior status. The Moon also wears dyed eagle feathers as headdress and collar, showing the feathers he must drop to follow The Sun, and revealing intuition and sometimes artifice. His cheeks are masked with short rainbow bars while an inverted tipi adorns his forehead and a true tipi, his chin. He is protected by a thick rainbow border with three feathers.

Suggested Interpretations Intuition. Deception. Twilight. Obscurity. Disillusionment. Danger. Bad influence. Ulterior motives. False friends. Selfishness. Deceit. Craftiness. Disgrace. Slander. Libel. Superficiality. Unknown enemies. Psychic ability revealed.

Reversed A minor deception recognized before damage is done. Trifling mistakes. Overcoming bad temptation. Gain without paying the price or peace gained at high cost. Taking advantage of someone.

Guardians The Moon's guardians are twin snakes.

XIX THE SUN — The Sun

Myth Father of the Twin War Gods—represented here by the two inverted and fringed medicine pouches—The Sun is a powerful god who affects most of The People's lives. It is The Sun who sent his sons, Monster Slayer and Born-of-Water (First Born), to fight the many monsters plaguing the earth, and it is The Sun who blesses the initiation ceremonies and naming dances. His primary concern is the welfare of The People. In order to best accomplish his goals, he lights the world and heats the seedlings, warms the land and bakes the rocks to useable hardness. Because he sees so much in his trips across the sky, he is a great source of information to many of the Yeis.

Symbology The Sun wears a horned headdress with long feathers and beads and wears cloth and bead earrings. His headdress is crowned with tremendous feathers and shafts of spears, while his collar is comprised of eagle feathers with sand and seeds painted on them. The central feather of the collar holds the sacred bean plant. He is protected by four rainbow bars.

Suggested Interpretations Satisfaction. Accomplishment. Contentment. Success. Favorable relationships. Love. Joy. Devotion. Unselfish sentiment. Engagement. A happy marriage. Pleasure in daily existence. A good friend. High spirits. Warmth. Sincerity. Pleasures derived from simple things. Achievement in the arts. Liberation.

Reversed Unhappiness. Loneliness. Possibly a broken engagement or marriage. Canceled plans. Triumph delayed although not necessarily completely lost. Clouded future.

Guardians None.

20 JUDGMENT
WATER CREATURES

XX JUDGMENT — WATER CREATURES

Myth Once, at the time of the Creation Story, Coyote was gambling with Water Monster. He won the game, and in return Water Monster gave him his very fine coat. When Coyote got home, he discovered Water Monster's twin babies in the pocket of the great coat. He decided that since the babies were sleeping and not any problem, he would keep them. This caused Water Monster to become very, very angry, and he sent a flood of water to punish The People. The People fled in terror and soon had to climb through a small hole in the sky where they emerged into the Fifth World. From that point on, four Water Creatures guard the waterways of the World. In traditional sandpainting, the four Water Creatures depicted represent Water Monster—Te-o-sol-hi.

Symbology Balancing the waterways of the world are four Water Creatures, two linked above and two also touching hands below. The waterways are twisted and confused.

These Yeis are all female in nature and the variation in dress reveal the different nature of balance. A tri-colored rainbow border with two feathers protect the Water Creatures in their difficult task. They are additionally protected by the two short rainbow bars inside the border.

Suggested Interpretations A life well lived, work well done. Awakening, renewal. Atonement. Judgment. The need to repent and forgive. The moment to account for the manner in which we have used our opportunities. Rejuvenation. Rebirth. Improvement. Development. Promotion. The desire for immortality. Legal judgment in one's favor. One should carefully consider how present actions affect other persons.

Reversed Delay. Disappointment. Failure to face facts. Indecision. Divorce. Procrastination. Theft. Alienation of affections.

Guardians None.

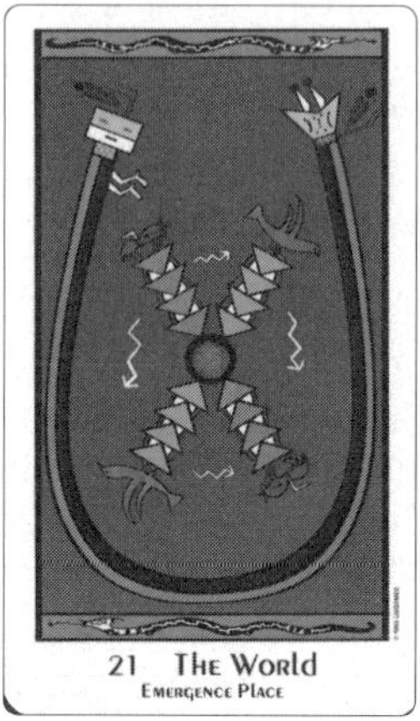

XXI THE WORLD — Emergence Place

Myth In the Creation Story, The People had to pass through several levels before arriving in the present or Fifth World. The small hole The People had to claw their way through to this world is still called The Emergence Place. The Navajo consider this a beautiful white world with green plants, red rocks, and blue water. In legend, The People know that since there were four worlds below this world, there must also be four worlds waiting above.

Symbology A yellow-masked and skirted Curved Rainbow Yei borders the world, offering it fierce protection. The world, depicted with sand in it, has corn-cloud rays stretching out from it. Two of the cloud tiers are capped with Buffalo People, the other two with Bird People, representing two of The People who managed to squeeze through into Fifth World. Crooked lightning lies in between the tiers but doesn't follow a particular pattern, showing the need for acceptance of change and the need to harmonize with the unknown.

Suggested Interpretations Attachment. Completion. Perfection. Ultimate change. The end result of all efforts. Success. Synthesis. Fulfillment. Capability. Triumph in undertakings. The rewards that come from hard work. Eternal life. Admiration of others. Travel. Arrival at cosmic consciousness.

Reversed Imperfection. Failure to complete the task one starts. Lack of vision. Fear of change or travel. Success yet to be won. Disappointment.

Guardians None.

4

THE MINOR ARCANA

The Minor Arcana, the basis of our modern-day playing cards, are divided into four equal suits of fourteen cards each. In The Santa Fe Tarot Deck, these four suits are Rainbows, Water, Lightning, and Buffalo. For those familiar with the Tarot, these four suits correspond respectively to Wands (Fire, Salamander, South); Cups (Water, Water Carrier, West); Swords (Air, Eagle, North); and Pentacles (Earth, Bull, East).

The Santa Fe Tarot Deck draws upon four of the Yei People groups to represent the suit cards: Rainbow Yeis for Rainbows, Thunder People for the suit of Lightning, Water Creatures for Water, and Buffalo People for the suit of Buffalo. These Yeis appear throughout the Ways or Chants of the Navajo, conferring the powerful forces of nature upon The People, teaching them magic, instructing them in healing, and most of all, aiding them to walk the Path of Beauty and Harmony.

SUIT OF RAINBOWS

When The People first arrived in the Fifth World, they knew nothing of the ways of the new land. They saw a river flowing before them and knew the Pueblos lived across it, but they didn't know anything of those people. The Pueblos, however, were willing enough to show The People how to plant corn, how to weave, and how to work pottery. One day the people heard many voices, and when they looked around they saw four gods approaching from the four directions. One of them, drawing near from the South, was Water Bearer Yei, curved like a rainbow, dressed in the colors of the sky. She smiled upon The People and made them welcome with her cool waters and gave them sweet cakes with honey to eat. Remember me, she told them. Remember.

The Rainbow People or Na'a-tse-elit Yei appear in many of the Ways of the Navajo. The most common form is found in the Mountainway Chant and shown with Rainbow bodies, curved or straight, elaborate headdresses, cloud rattles and corn-tassels. They often appear in pairs, like double-rainbows. A Rainbow Yei is often used to protect the sacred sandpainting, encircling the vulnerable southern, western and northern sides, making certain the painting always 'faces' east.

Generally, the Rainbow People are considered a hasty, gift-giving, loving people, capable of great harmony and peace, though occasionally they stray into areas that don't really concern them.

The border color of The Santa Fe Tarot Deck's Rainbow suit is deep rose, and the background color of the four court cards is also a deep rose. The remaining ten cards of the suit each have a lighter rose background. The design at the top of the cards is taken from one of the Wide Ruins Navajo, Arizona rug border designs.

The suit of Rainbows corresponds directly to Wands or Rods, and are generally equated with the element of fire. The temperament of Wands is said to be sanguine, and this directly equates to the personality of the Rainbow People. The Rainbow suit most often relates to those people who have light-colored hair and blue or green eyes.

The rainbow raised up with me.
Through the middle of broad fields,
The rainbow returned with me.
Where my house is visible,
The rainbow returned with me.
Navajo

KING OF RAINBOWS — Big Rainbow Yei

Myth On the day when Father Sky and Big Thunder first raised their voices in the fourth world, they were so happy with the sound and light they created that they enjoined their voices once again. This time they gave birth to a man and a woman and they were called Rainbow People. Big Rainbow Yei looked down at his fine, colorful garments and was pleased. He looked across the sky, saw his wife, Rainbow Woman, and his sons, Black Rainbow Yei, and Little Rainbow, and was content. He gathered his newborn family and, after surveying the world, decided to rest upon Rain Mountain. Though he travels far and wide, he still makes his home upon the top of Rain Mountain and is often called Rain Mountain Chief.

Symbology One of the curved Rainbow People, Big Rainbow Yei holds a bow and arrow in his left hand and a large prayer stick in his right, while a smaller, prayer stick with fringe dangles from his elbow. His skirt is decorated with seeds and sand, indicating the point where a rainbow touches the ground. He wears an elaborate weasel headdress and feather earrings.

SUGGESTED INTERPRETATIONS An honest and conscientious person. Mature. Wise. Devoted. Friendly. Sympathetic. Educated. A gentleman. Generally married. Fatherly. Sometimes can be hasty.

REVERSED Severity. Austerity. Excessive and exaggerated ideas. Dogmatic. Deliberate. Intolerant, prejudiced.

GUARDIANS Twin Black Suns flank Big Rainbow Yei instead of protecting the vulnerable eastern edge of the sandpainting. Big Rainbow Yei is the bridge that all can travel, and as such, needs no protection.

QUEEN OF RAINBOWS — RAINBOW WOMAN

Myth Rainbow Woman sat weaving a beautiful blanket in her home on Striped Mountain when she saw two small children, a boy and a girl, standing outside the door of her hogan. The children looked cold and afraid, and when they saw she wasn't weaving any longer, but was looking at them, they tried to run away. She cast a skein of her wool after them, wrapping them in richly-colored clothing. She asked the children what they wanted at the home of Rainbow Woman and they began to cry. 'We want nothing,' they said. 'We are lost and cannot find our way home.' With that, Rainbow Woman cast a strand of her multi-colored wool across the sky. 'Follow the trail of beauty,' she said, 'and you will find your way back.' The children did as she told them and soon found themselves in the loving arms of their worried parents. The People knew from that day onward that the rainbow was the trail to follow when seeking something lost.

Symbology Rainbow Woman wears an elaborate weasel headdress with blue feathers over a peaked cap. One of the curved Rainbow People, Rainbow Woman wears a blouse of yellow and blue. Weasel rattles hang from her arms and she carries bullroarers in each Earth circle hand. A jeweled and decorated medicine pouch dangles from one hand. Her skirt is a striped green and black pattern, showing her affinity with her home, Striped Mountain. A single-banded red Rainbow Guardian wearing a weasel headdress and carrying both a medicine pouch and a prayer stick with clouds upon it encircles Rainbow Woman, but could almost be said to be her mirror image, the double rainbow that brings good luck.

Suggested Interpretations A sympathetic and understanding woman. Fruitful in mind and body. Loves nature and her home. Friendly. Loving. Chaste. Practical. Charm and grace. Hospitality. Sincere interest in others.

Reversed Domineering, obstinate, revengeful. Someone who is likely to turn suddenly against another without cause. Jealousy. Deceit. Possible infidelity. Unstable emotions. Fickleness. Resistance. Opposition.

Guardians Twin Sun guardians protect Rainbow Woman.

Knight of Rainbows
Black Rainbow Yei

KNIGHT OF RAINBOWS — Black Rainbow Yei

Myth Once a man came to Striped Mountain. For three days he made his home at the base of the mountain, and for three nights he lit a campfire, sending sparks high into the night sky and smoke curling up the side of the mountain. In his hand he carried a small rock crystal, and as his fire burned he thought he could see glimpses of a fearful Yei-tso, a monster come to devour him. In truth, what he saw was Black Rainbow Yei, who had come down from Striped Mountain to see who dared disturb his peace with smoke and sparks of fire. At the dawn's light he revealed himself and demanded the man leave, but the man, though he feared this angry Yei greatly, said he couldn't leave. He was seeking his wife who had been stolen from him. Black Rainbow Yei could see the man wouldn't leave without his wife, so he sought her himself, and brought her back on a curved rainbow. Before he would give the stolen wife back to her husband, he demanded the man put out the fire. This is why young men in trouble seek out Black Rainbow

Yei, lighting fires for three nights, and then dousing them, never to look for them again.

Symbology Black Rainbow Yei is dressed in black and yellow warrior colors. He carries an arrow in one hand and has a spare in his skirt. He also carries a small red prayer stick. A large prayer stick hovers just beyond him, as if showing that he will have to put something down in order to take it. His headdress is comprised of a single mountain-sheep horn, scarves, feathers, and flint. He is perched atop Striped Mountain where all rainbows are said to end. A single inverted black cloud hangs in the sky behind him. His leggings hold zigzag lightning, and his feet, water signs.

Suggested Interpretations A journey. Advancement into the unknown. A young man, possibly a warrior. He can be a generous friend or love, but can also be easily angered, even cruel. Alteration. Flight. A person who is hasty in all he does. Absence. Change of residence.

Reversed Interruption. Unexpected change. Quarreling. Breakup of personal relationships. Rupture.

Guardians None.

Page of Rainbows
Little Rainbow

PAGE OF RAINBOWS — Little Rainbow

Myth When the Rainbow People first settled in their home on Striped Mountain (except for Big Rainbow Yei, who lived on Rain Mountain) Little Rainbow found little to make himself useful. He was treated like a child, not allowed to journey or behave at all like the supernatural he was. Then, one night, a man came to him. The man seemed surprised. He said he was there in a vision only. The man wanted to know many things; so did Little Rainbow. Together they traveled without leaving. They went far and wide, and always returned by morning. This is how The People travel without leaving home and how a medicine man journeys to the spirit world.

Symbology Little Rainbow is one of the straight Rainbow People. He's dressed in blue, black, and red. His skirt is striped showing his link with his home, Striped Mountain. He carries a large blue prayer stick in both hands, as if carrying it with extreme care. His headdress is squared with a single flagged feather and feather earrings. He stands upon two rainbow bars. Inverted clouds flank him on both sides.

Suggested Interpretations A faithful, loyal person. An envoy. Emissary. Trusted friend. A stranger with good intentions. A consistent person. A bearer of important news. An important message.

Reversed Indecision. Reluctance. Instability. A gossip. Bearer of bad tidings. A heart-breaker. Displeasure. A person who could be cruel, unstable. Domineering spirit.

Guardians Twin cloud rattles serve as Little Rainbow's guardians, conferring the ability to choose wisely.

TEN OF RAINBOWS

Symbology A curved Rainbow Yei is also portrayed here with a slightly bent skirt. The head is bowed, facing downward. He carries five blue prayer sticks in each Earth circle hand. Instead of conferring power and protection, they are a burden. He stands between two mountain ranges covered with sand. His dress is yellow and slate-blue, showing his warrior status. He wears scarves as a headdress and a single feather extends beyond them.

Divinatory Meanings Pressure. Problems soon to be resolved. Striving to meet a goal or to maintain a certain level or position. Possibly using power for selfish ends.

Reversed Difficulties. Intrigues. A traitor. Deceiver. Subterfuge. Some losses will occur. Separation.

NINE OF RAINBOWS

Symbology A female curved Rainbow Yei has a slightly bent black skirt though her blouse is red and blue. She wears a single white scarf as a headdress. She holds a single red prayer stick in one hand, while the other is empty. Four red prayer sticks behind her seem about to strike her, while four in front of her block her path. She stands in a valley in the mountains, upon a stylized version of Big Fly.

Divinatory Meanings Expectation of difficulties and changes. Anticipation. Hidden enemies. Deception. Discipline. Order. A pause in a current struggle. Eventual victory might occur, but only after steady force has been applied.

Reversed Obstacles. Adversity. Problems. Delays. Disaster. Barriers to overcome. Weakness. Ill health.

EIGHT OF RAINBOWS

Symbology A variation of the Whirling Logs sandpainting, sometimes called the Swastika painting, one large and one small prayer stick rest upon each extending bar of a pair of crossed straight rainbows. They spiral in a clockwise motion, four prayer sticks on the red bar, four on the blue. Red and blue feathers decorate each end of the crossed bars.

Divinatory Meanings Great hope. Swift activity. Sudden progress or movement. Speed. Hastily made decisions. Too rapid advancement. Messages, letters of love. Approach to a goal. Journey by air.

Reversed Thorns of dispute. Jealousy. Harassment. Stagnation in business or personal affairs. Domestic quarrels.

Seven of Rainbows

SEVEN OF RAINBOWS

Symbology A curved male Rainbow Yei with a straight skirt stands alone, as though having survived a struggle. He holds a long red prayer stick with both hands, not worried about the six he doesn't hold. He wears a red and blue blouse and his face mask is white and orange. The orange is repeated in the center of skirt, reflecting his affinity with the Earth. He has zigzag lightning leggings and stands upon a rainbow bar.

Divinatory Meanings Victory through courage. Success. Gain. Overwhelming odds surmounted. Advantage. Competition in business or trade, but possessing certainty of reward.

Reversed Consternation. Anxiety. Embarrassment. Hesitancy causing losses. Perplexity. Some pretense involved.

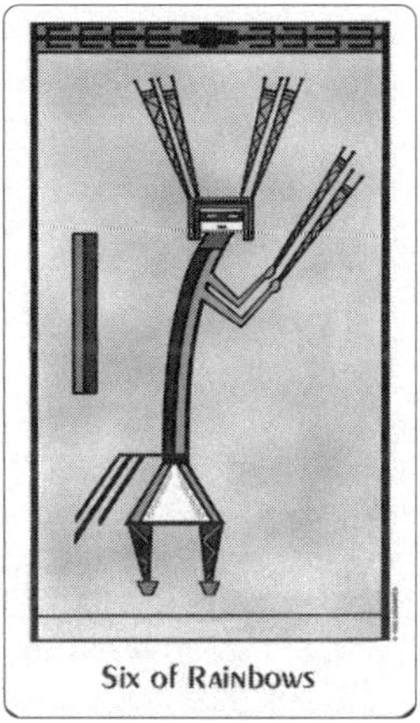

SIX OF RAINBOWS

Symbology A female curved Rainbow Yei wears a headdress containing four prayer sticks while holding two others in each hand. The prayer sticks are all earth-colored as is part of her dress, the zigzag lightning in her leggings, and her feet. The remainder of her dress is blue, with a white peak in her skirt. Her feet contain sand, showing her affinity with the earth. A rainbow bar stands behind her, protecting her.

Divinatory Meanings Conquest. Triumph. Good news. Advancement. Expectation. Desires realized as a result of efforts. Victory after strife. Friends are helpful.

Reversed Indefinite delay. Fear. Apprehension. Disloyalty. Superficial benefit. Inconclusive gain.

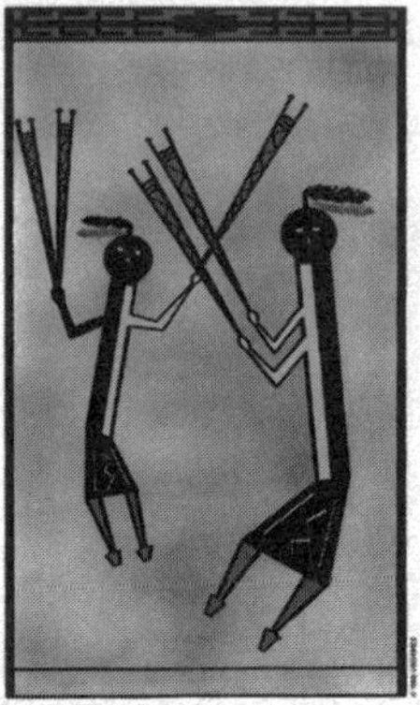

Five of Rainbows

FIVE OF RAINBOWS

Symbology Two bent warrior Rainbow Yeis battle each other for possession of the other's prayer sticks. Each has enough, but both wish for more. Both figures are dressed in warrior colors, yellow and black, and have yellow straight and zigzag lightning in their otherwise unadorned skirts. The smaller figure has two red prayer sticks in one hand, one in the other. The larger figure only carries two, one in each hand. They both have red legs and feet, and are wearing black and red feathers as headdresses.

Divinatory Meanings Unsatisfied desires. Struggle. Labor. Violent strife. Obstacles. Lawsuits. Rashness in competition.

Reversed Trickery. Contradictions. Complexity. Involvement. Caution against indecision. Victory after surmounting obstacles.

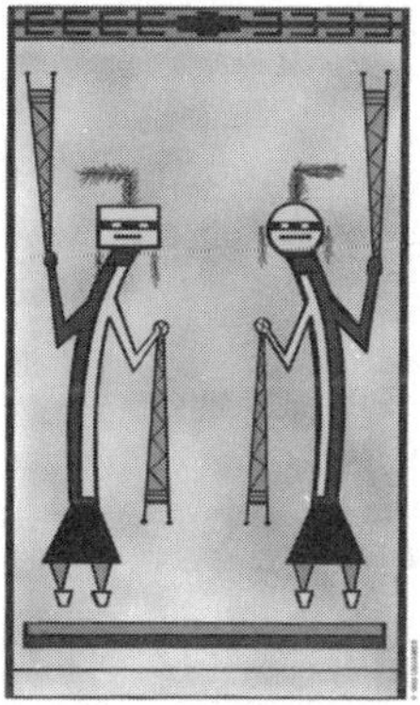

Four of Rainbows

FOUR OF RAINBOWS

Symbology Male and female curved Rainbow Yeis stand upon a long rainbow bar holding their prayer sticks both upward and downward. In identical posture, both have the blue hands, marked with the Earth circle, holding the prayer sticks aloft, while the yellow Earth circle-marked hand allows the prayer stick to dangle. Dressed in semi-warrior colors, yellow and blue, with warrior masks, these Yeis create an image of harmony and balance.

Divinatory Meanings Romance. Society. Harmony. Newly acquired prosperity. Tranquility. The fruits of labor. Rest after strife. Possible indication of marriage.

Reversed Loss of full tranquility. Unfulfilled romance. Insecurity. Tarnished beauty. Incomplete happiness. Some peace, some harmony, though not as much as in upright position.

Three of Rainbows

THREE OF RAINBOWS

Symbology This female curved Rainbow Yei holds two earth-toned prayer sticks in one hand, one in the other, as though announcing her success. She wears a complex headdress adorned with three blue feathers on top and six feathers as earrings. She also has two feathers over her skirt sashes. She is dressed in a red and black blouse with a striped orange skirt and white leggings with blue zigzag lightning. Her feet are red with black lightning. A small rainbow bar stands beside her.

Divinatory Meanings Realization of hope. Established strength, wealth and power. Caution against pride and arrogance. Partnership. Practical knowledge. Business acumen. Enterprise. Negotiations. Trade. Commerce.

Reversed Assistance with an ulterior motive. Diminishing adversity. Wealth might slip away.

Two of Rainbows

TWO OF RAINBOWS

Symbology A male curved Rainbow Yei holds two blue prayer sticks in one hand and an undecorated Black Sun in the other. His red and blue blouse is decorated with contrasting red and blue fringe, while his red skirt has a rectangular white panel inset, representing his proud nature. He wears a single crooked feather as his headdress and a band of red as a mask. His feet are two blue single-barred rainbows.

Divinatory Meanings Mature individual. Ruler. Attainment of goals and needs. Boldness. Courage in undertakings. A dominant personality. The employment of scientific methods. Could indicate a proud and unforgiving nature. A certain coolness.

Reversed Sadness. Trouble. Restraint caused by others. Loss of faith. Surprise. Restlessness.

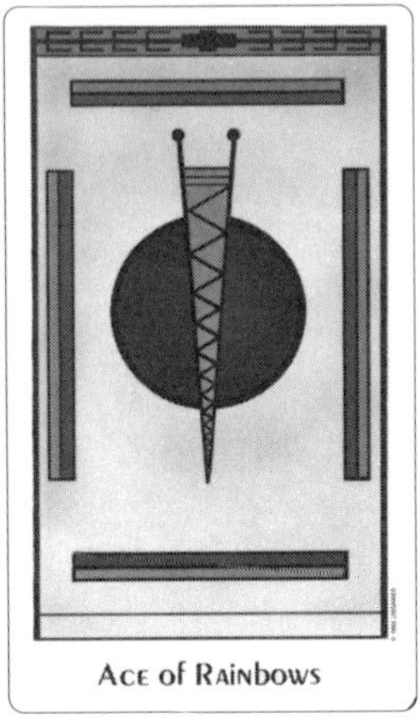

ACE OF RAINBOWS

Symbology A single red prayer stick rests against the Earth circle. This sandpainting design is bordered with four red and blue straight rainbows offering protection and safety. In purest terms, the prayer stick relates to the spirit, the Earth circle to the world, the rainbows a bridge between the two.

Divinatory Meanings Creation. Beginning. Invention. Start of an undertaking. Fortune. Enterprise. Gain. Could indicate the beginning of a journey or adventure. Inheritance. Birth of a child. Beginning of a meaningful experience. Escapade.

Reversed False start. Cloudy outlook. Unrealized goal. Decadence. Empty existence. Vexation. Cancellation of plans.

SUIT OF WATER

One day, just after arriving in the Fifth World, and still tired from the journey through the Emergence Place, The People came upon Water Monster Old Man. In his kindness, he gave them collected water, and Water's child. But The People had nothing to carry the water in, so they journeyed further and came upon a place called The-interior-of-a-pot, the home of Pot Carrier (a blister beetle). He did not want to give them a pot. They took their leave of him and met Old Man Toad in his home called One-gazes-upon-the-cornfield. He gave them jewels to take back to Pot Carrier, who then gave them a pot so they could hold the water Water Monster Old Man had given them. Thus The People came to know that keeping water would be a difficult but satisfying thing.

The Water People, Water Creatures, and Water Monsters figure in a multitude of the five hundred recorded and known sandpaintings and are said to have existed in many of the Ways which are now considered extinct. The Water People govern the waterways of the Earth, from large to very small bodies of water.

The Water folk are known for their considerable strength, their sense of responsibility, and for their gaiety. In many ways, they are one of the keepers of this world, for without water there can be no life.

The suit of Water relates in the tarot as Cups, and the point on the compass generally assigned to it is West. The suit most often corresponds with matters of the heart and the home. While the water symbol is often regarded as phlegmatic, newer interpretations correlate the sound of water to the temperament of the suit: when gurgling, pleasant; when roaring, dangerous.

The Santa Fe Tarot Deck's Water suit is bordered in dark blue with lighter blue and turquoise backgrounds for the court and ten suit cards. The top border design of the suit of Water is the swirled pattern most easily identified with the Papago Indian, but also used by their nearby neighbors the Mohave Apache.

Running water, running water
I hear your voice calling my name
I hear your voice call my name
I hear your voice.

Running water, running water
I hear your roar.
I hear your roar
As I am carried to the sky.
As I am carried to the sky.
Navajo

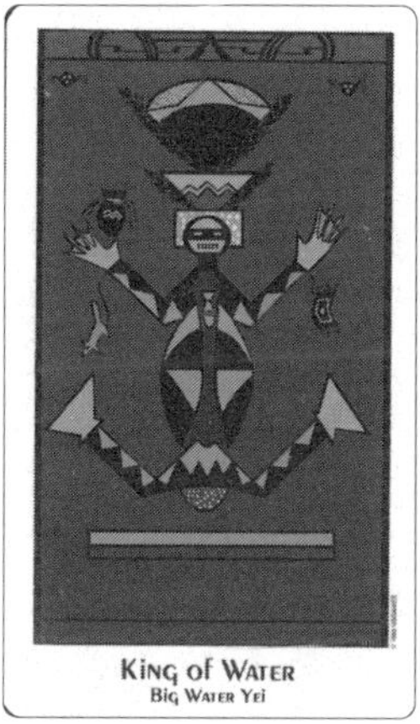

KING OF WATER — Big Water Yei

Myth Big Water Yei, or Te-o-sol-hi, is a powerful Yei-tso, one of the monsters that roam the Worlds. However, because he is so powerful, he holds qualities both terrible and wonderful. When Coyote stole Big Water Yei's twin children, he sent a huge flood that drove The People into the Fifth World. In an act of justice, however, he sent four of his finest Water Creatures to guard the waterways of the new world so that The People would find happiness and the Path of Beauty. He is careful of The People who look to him: Frog, Otter, Dragonfly, Big Fly, and Fish. He knows that all creatures once were in his domain yet is content that some have gained wings or legs and now live elsewhere. Big Water Yei causes the rivers to flow and is responsible for them.

Symbology Water Creatures generally resemble the Father Sky/Mother Earth figures when represented in sandpaintings. Big Water Yei is no exception. From his webbed hands dangle a weasel pouch and a medicine bundle. In one hand he holds the sacred water jug. His body is decorated in red-orange and black showing his chameleon-like agility. His tail holds the constellations, though in some versions the spotted tail signifies the sea foam. His headdress is very elaborate, double-tiered, feathered and jeweled. A rainbow bar supports him.

Suggested Interpretations This man is skilled in both law and trade. He could be connected with a church or a worldly institution. He has a willingness to accept responsibility. Creativity. Learned person. Professional. Scientist. A considerate person, kind and reliable. Liberal manner. Artist. Interest in the arts and sciences. Generosity.

Reversed A powerful man, but likely to be crafty or violent. A fierce nature under a deceptive exterior. Artistic temperament. Double dealing. Scandal. Loss. Ruin. Injustice.

Guardians Sun and Moon guardians offer their protection.

Queen of Water
Water Woman

QUEEN OF WATER — Water Woman

Myth It is told that First Man owned a mirage stone and a living rock crystal. He also owned Water's sparkling rock and Water's foam. Of this, he said one day, shall two persons be made. Talking God helped him with the words while First Man gathered many items, blue mist, the song of blue swifts, amniotic fluid, and strange and wonderful material. After sanctifying these things, two persons fell out of them, a man and a woman. The man he called Mountain Woman and the woman he named Water Woman. He told Water Woman she would always be in control of collected waters, and of the small ponds—Water's Child. She was also placed in governance of the things that live under the water. Water Woman was placed upon the north side of the Earth with Navajo Mountain as her headrest, Much Wool Peak as a cane. She was content in her task and still cares for The People who came to live beside the waters she tends.

Symbology Water Woman carries single curved rainbow bars in one webbed hand and a sacred water jug in the other clutched fist. She also has feathers trailing from each hand, her legs, and from the uppermost tier of her cloud-shaped headdress. Her body is black with a water symbol painted on it. Her center is Big Fly, signifying both her beauty and her ability to mediate. Her tail is dotted with sea foam or constellations and is fringed for beauty. Her water jug is black with water symbols upon it.

Suggested Interpretations A woman who is able to manifest what she dreams. She is a good wife and mother, honest, loyal, and devoted. A warm-hearted and fair person. Beloved and adored. Good friend. Practical. Loving and intelligent. Gift of vision. Success, happiness and pleasure are also indicated.

Reversed Dishonesty. Unreliability. Vice. An intelligent person, but not to be counted on. Immorality.

Guardians None.

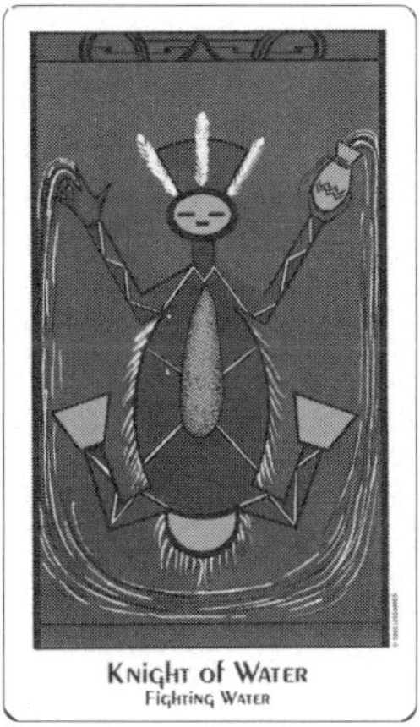

KNIGHT OF WATER — Fighting Water

Myth Fighting Water, also known as Born-for-Water or First Son, is the twin brother of Monster Slayer, and son of Changing Woman and The Sun. It seems The Sun, knowing that most monsters were born of him, resolved to have sons which would fight their Yei-tso brothers. The Sun tricked Changing Woman into bedding with him, coming to her when he was invisible at night, and disappearing at first light. The Sun aided in Changing Woman's difficult birth and afterward wrapped his twin sons in unique warrior garments. Fighting Water he wrapped in blue flint, dark flint, and serrated flint. He was draped in blue clouds and was carried into the dawn light. After traveling many miles with his brother, and killing many of their brother monsters, Fighting Water went to his father, The Sun. When offered riches, land, many horses, Fighting Water turned them all down. It seems all he wanted was a place of peace. He was given tribute and placed in the center of Hot Springs and was thereafter given control of all the warm waters.

Symbology Fighting Water is wearing the blue flint his father gave him. The lightning bolts that presaged his birth are woven into his dress. A modified version of Big Fly comprises the center of his body, conferring grace and beauty. Water flows from his sacred water jug to his webbed fingertips and back again, showing his ability to sustain the waters. His headdress is made of three eagle feathers across a crown of blue flint. His dress is fringed with white flint.

Suggested Interpretations An invitation or opportunity may soon arise. Arrival. Approach. Advancement. Attraction. Inducement. Appeal. A graceful man who is a dreamer. Challenge. Proposal.

Reversed Subtlety. Artifice. Trickery. A sly and cunning person. A person capable of swindling. Any proposition should be carefully considered now.

Guardians None.

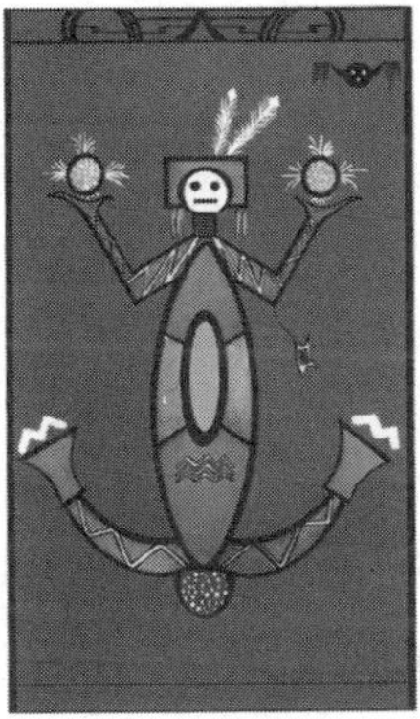

PAGE OF WATER
Water Child

PAGE OF WATER — WATER CHILD

MYTH Some tales refer to Water Child as the son of Water Woman, where others simply have him already there, but all agree he remains under the guidance of Water Woman, for he is but a smaller version of her inland waters. As a youth, Water Child loved to play and would often steal out of the small ponds and scatter droplets of precious water upon the plants and trees that grew nearby. But he became sad when after placing droplets of water across their hogans and blankets, The Sun would steal his gifts before The People could gather them. Finally, with age, Water Child learned that he could safely sprinkle his droplets of water at two times of the year—in the days when The Sun drifted further away, before the days of severe cold; and then again, when The Sun drew closer, but before The Sun would begin baking the earth anew. During those two times of year Water Child will again steal out to proffer his water gifts for The People. And this is why The People have the dew in the fall and spring.

Symbology Water Child holds a water gourd decorated with feathers in each of his hands. These water gourds also appear as modified Zia symbols, the Native American version of The Sun. The speckles on the gourds represent the droplets of dew that Water Child offers every fall and spring. A medicine pouch dangles from one arm. His arms and legs are decorated with lightning and he wears two white feathers on his squared headdress. Corn earrings dangle from his headdress as well. A water symbol rests below a modified Big Fly and both his feet are marked with water symbols.

Suggested Interpretations A youthful person of a studious and intent nature. Can be reflective, meditative. He is loyal and possesses a spirit willing to offer services and efforts toward a specific goal. Can be helpful. Can also be given to flights of imagination.

Reversed Inclination. Deviation. Susceptibility. Temporary distraction. Seduction. A flatterer. A deception may soon be uncovered. Unpleasant news may arrive.

Guardians A single Moon guardian aids Water Child in his quest to present dew to The People.

Ten of Water

TEN OF WATER

Symbology Two Water People, male and female, support each other in joy. In the female's webbed and open palm an Earth circle can be seen. Both are wearing Turtle shells for protection and lightning bolts across their shoulders for strength. Both male and female headdresses and tails are adorned with blue spruce boughs. In each outstretched hand, they hold an inverted sacred water jug. Balanced upon the jug is a curved rainbow and above it are eight inverted water jugs. Their hands and the rainbows prevent the water from spilling out. Two curved rainbow bars rest beneath them.

Divinatory Meanings Perfection of love. Great friendship. Peacemaking. Home. Joy. Pleasure. Peace. Love. Contentment. Good family. Honor. Esteem. Virtue.

Reversed Loss of friendship. Unhappiness. Family quarrel. Pettiness. Rage. Difference of opinion. Wasted love.

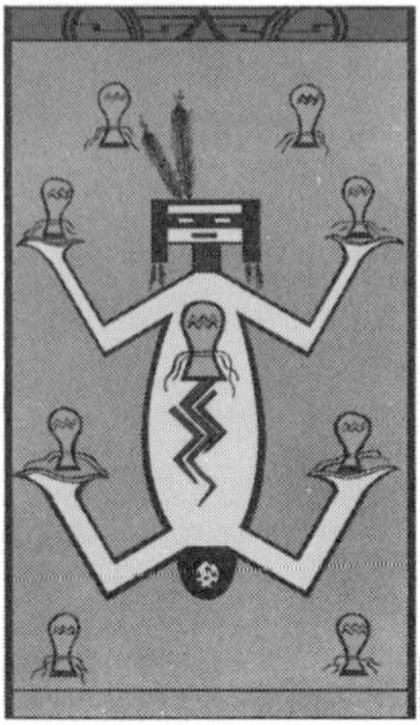

Nine of Water

NINE OF WATER

Symbology While the sacred water jugs are all inverted here, they are kept from spilling free by the magic of fulfillment. This Water Yei has enough to share, enough to spill. He supports four inverted jugs on hands and feet, and two hover above him while the remaining two rest beneath. The final sacred water jug can be found in the Water Yei's body. It, too, is inverted, but spills stylized water and sacred plants free across him, enriching him.

Divinatory Meanings Success. Material attainment. Advantage. Well-being. Abundance. Satisfaction. Good health. Difficulties surmounted.

Reversed Mistakes. Material loss. Imperfections. Misplaced trust. False freedom. Overindulgence in food or drink. Opposition. Differences.

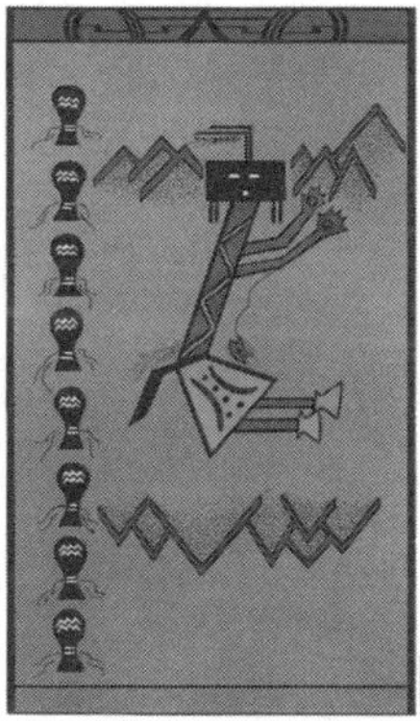

Eight of Water

EIGHT OF WATER

Symbology A bent female Yei appears trapped between two mountain ranges. Her medicine pouch is empty and she can't reach the eight stacked jugs of sacred water. And if she did, it would afford her little delight for the jugs are inverted and the water has all fallen out. Her dress is red with zigzag lightning. Her hands and feet are the symbols of the Water People, but her bent direction indicates her failure or disappointment.

Divinatory Meanings Discontinuance of effort. Disappointment, possibly in love. Journeying from place to place without fulfillment. Abandonment of previous plans. Shyness. Modesty. Abandoned success.

Reversed Effort continued until full success is attained. Festivity. Gaiety. Possibility of a new love.

SEVEN OF WATER

Symbology One of the male Water People holds both hands upright, but supports nothing in them. Beside him a cloud tower has contained six sacred water jugs and keeps them from spilling all their precious liquid even though they are inverted. However, one jug hovers alone, inverted, with nothing to prevent its spillage. An inverted sun guardian guards that which the Water Person strives to hold. A rainbow bar decorated with feathers rests beneath both the Water Person and the cloud tower.

Divinatory Meanings Fantasy. Imagination working overtime. Daydreams. Foolish whims. Wishful thinking. Illusionary success. Self-deception.

Reversed Desire. New determination. Strong willpower. A goal nearly attained. Intelligent choice. Good resolutions.

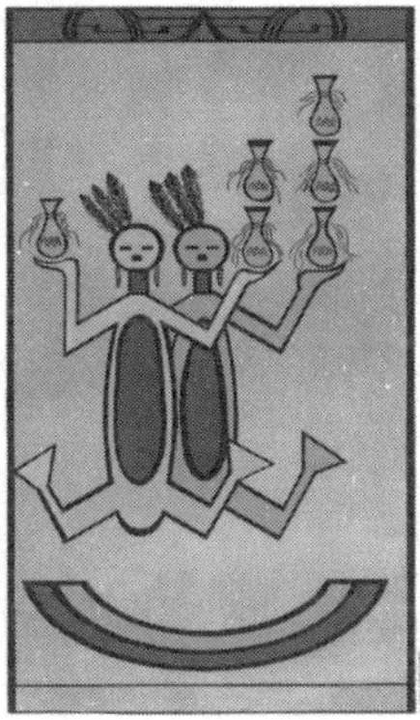

Six of Water

SIX OF WATER

Symbology Twin brothers hold three sacred jugs in harmonious balance. They are different, but essentially the same. Each Water Yei wears blue spruce headdresses and loop earrings. One of the Yeis is a darker reflection of the other. A curved rainbow links them together and protects them.

Divinatory Meanings Memories. Past influences. Things that have vanished. Childhood passed. Nostalgia. Faded images. Pleasant memories. This card can indicate new friendships or a gift from an admirer. New opportunities might arise.

Reversed The future. Opportunities ahead. Coming events. New vistas. Plans that may fail. That which will shortly arrive. There is a possibility of a gift or inheritance that arises from some dealing in the past.

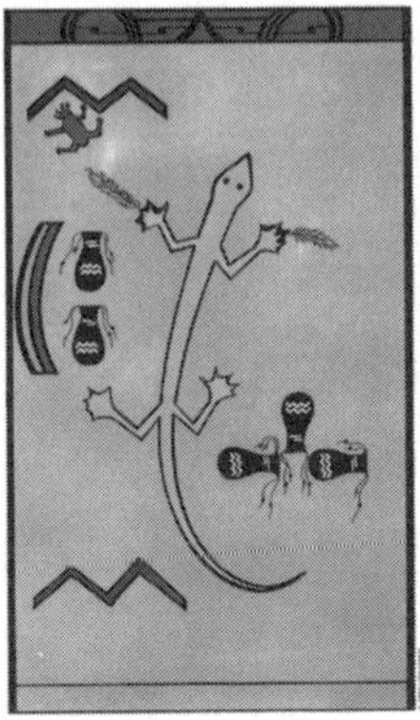

Five of Water

FIVE OF WATER

Symbology One of the Water Creatures, this Water Lizard travels from mountain range to mountain range in search of something he doesn't understand. All seems empty to him, because of the three spilled sacred water jugs beside him. He doesn't notice that right behind him are two full jugs protected by a curved rainbow. Another Water Creature is trapped in the high mountain range, but is not the source of the Water Lizard's search, though could be the cause of the sorrow he feels.

Divinatory Meanings Loss but with something left over. Regret. Friendship without real meaning. Marriage without real love. Inheritance may come but at some pain. Incomplete union or partnership.

Reversed Hopeful outlook. Favorable expectations. New alliances. Affinity. Return of an old friend or loved one. Reunion.

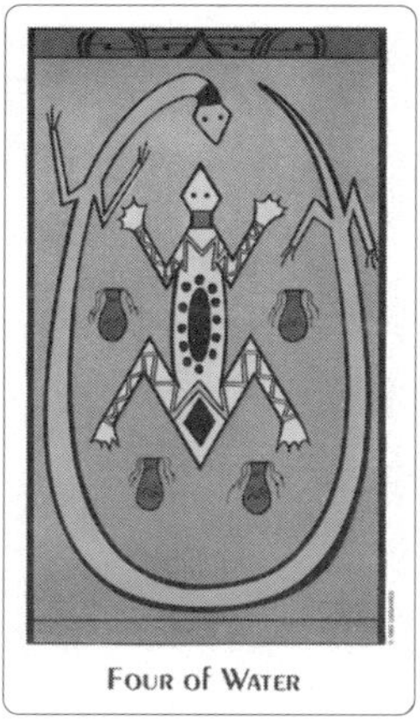

FOUR OF WATER

Symbology A Water Lizard surrounds a Spotted Water Creature, trapping him. While the Spotted Water Creature cannot escape, he has four sacred water jugs hovering near him. The trapped creature is spotted with the seeds of life and decorated with zigzag lightning. His webbed hands and feet are empty.

Divinatory Meanings Weariness. Aversion. Disgust. Disappointment. Bitter experience. A stationary period in life. A time to reevaluate one's life. Kindness from others. Emotions turned inward.

Reversed New possibilities. New relationships. New approaches to old problems. New knowledge. Stretching out of a period of solitude and reflection.

Three of Water

THREE OF WATER

Symbology A large Earth circle in the shape of The Sun or Zia supports three full sacred water jugs. The Earth circle is divided into four equal parts representing the four seasons and the four elements. In each quadrant of the circle are the symbols for water, home, food, and air. Dyed Eagle feathers stretch from the Earth circle like rays of The Sun. Decorated smoke pipes complete the sandpainting, signifying success.

Divinatory Meanings Resolution of a problem. Conclusion. Solace. Healing. Satisfactory result. Fulfillment. Compromise. Good fortune, victory. Hospitality. Pleasure.

Reversed Excessive pleasures. Overabundance. Superfluity. Loss of prestige. Delays. Lack of appreciation. Pleasure could turn to pain, success to ruin.

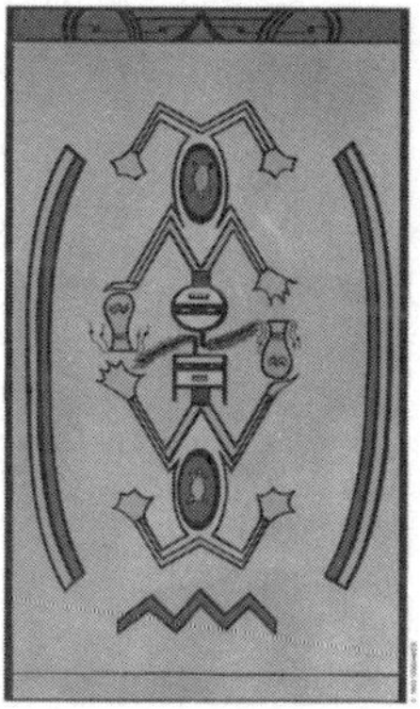

Two of Water

TWO OF WATER

Symbology A male and female Water Creature meet each other, twin images, opposites but united by touch and spirit. Tiny otters adorn each stomach in an oval shape, the symbol for the egg, the eternal fertility of both male and female. Each holds a single sacred water jar, and by positioning, what falls from hers, he catches; and what he spills, she holds. Curved rainbows flank each side. Both wear single-feathered headdresses that almost intertwine, but, in fact, do not touch.

Divinatory Meanings Love. Harmony of the masculine and the feminine. Friendship beginning or renewed. Passion. Union. Engagement. Understanding. Co-operation. Partnership. Marriage.

Reversed Unsatisfactory love. False friendship. Troubled relationship. Divorce. Separation. Crossed desires. Opposition. Misunderstanding.

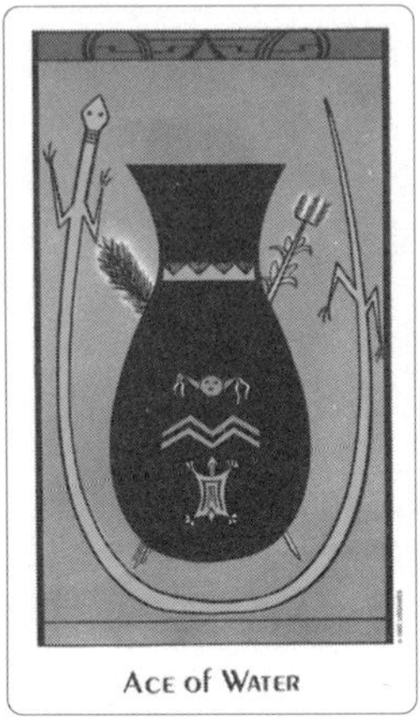

ACE OF WATER

Symbology Water Lizard protects a large sacred water jug, perhaps the very one carried by Water Bearer Yei before The People emerged in the fifth world. The jug is a rich black and has a mountain bar at its neck. Moon, Water, and Bat are drawn upon its front while the sacred plants of tobacco and corn cross the jug from behind.

Divinatory Meanings The beginning of all good things. Joy. Great abundance. Fulfillment. Perfection. Beauty and pleasure. The spirit in action. Fertility. Opulence. Productiveness. Goodness overflowing. Favorable outlook.

Reversed False or unrequited love. Clouded joy. Change. Erosion. Instability. Sterility. False heart. Inconsistency. Reluctance to nurture love.

SUIT OF LIGHTNING

Out of the darkness, the empty black of the dark world, the voice of Father Sky and Big Thunder could be heard. Big Thunder released lightning from his powerful wings. A brilliant arc of fire lit the night, illuminating the heavens, revealing the depth of Father Sky. Big Thunder's voice gathered strength as the air rushed in to follow the trail of the fire in the sky, and his roar was heard across the land. Father Sky embraced the voice and the colors, and in their joined happiness at their creation, rays of light and color appeared and the birth of Rainbow Guardians occurred.

The Thunder People are very powerful, and therefore are potentially dangerous gods. Lightning often shoots from their wings and feet, and many times they will have sky or rainbow symbols inside them. Easily angered, the Thunder People were prone to capturing or kidnapping unsuspecting heroes of Navajo folklore, only to exact a terrible punishment on them for having dared flirt with the Thunder's wrath. However, for all their uncertain temperament, the Thunder People don't hold grudges for very long and will usually reward the long-suffering hero/heroine with a healing way or chant.

While found in almost all the Ways, the origins of the Thunder People can be seen in sandpaintings from the Shootingway, Hailway, and Mountainway. These are the ways that primarily focus upon such disasters as earthquakes, hailstorms, cyclones, hurricanes, and other catastrophes brought about by man's ignorance and blundering on the Path of Beauty.

The suit of Lightning is bordered by a black and orange patterned design taken from one of the earlier Navajo rug patterns. The background of the Lightning suit is yellow, signifying the Thunder People's warrior-like nature.

Lightning in the Santa Fe Tarot Deck is equivalent to the suit of Swords and relates to the element of Air.

I wonder if the lone eyes are watching me?
I wonder if the lone eyes are watching me?
I am he who has killed the monsters.
The lightning is before me.
The lightning is behind me.
All is beautiful before me.
All is beautiful behind me.
All is beautiful around me.
NAVAJO

King of Lightning
Big Thunder Yei

KING OF LIGHTNING — Big Thunder Yei

Myth One day, after escaping the wrath of his parents, Rainboy came upon a beautiful house colored like the Rainbow. He was very hungry and tired from his travels, but when he spied a beautiful woman weaving a colored blanket, he also became conscious of his raggedness and tried to run away. She caught him and kept him. Rainboy didn't know she was married and that he'd incurred the wrath of Big Thunder Yei, who sent a great bolt of his lightning and killed Rainboy. Big Fly persuaded the other Thunders to help heal Rainboy, rousing Big Thunder Yei to fury at their intervention. Luckily, a peace was made and Big Thunder Yei forgave Rainboy. This is when Big Thunder Yei and all the Thunder People taught the ceremony of the Hail Chant.

Symbology Big Thunder, or Ikne'etso, is shown here with crooked lightning shooting from his wings and feet. The many rainbow bars in his dress reveal his great strength and compassion. He wears an elaborate weasel headdress (common among Mountainway sandpaintings). He carries a medicine pouch from each wing.

SUGGESTED INTERPRETATIONS A man who may be a lawyer or judge. Decisive. He gives wise counsel and is as firm in his enmities as he is in his friendships. Powerful. Authoritative. Controlled. Commanding. A professional man. Highly analytical person. Justness. Force. Superiority. A person having many ideas, thoughts and designs.

REVERSED A person who may pursue a matter to ruin. Cruelty. Conflict. Selfishness. Sadism. One who causes unnecessary disturbance and sadness. Perversity.

GUARDIANS Two bat guardians, messengers of the night, are above his head. Bat is one of the go-betweens in the peace between the Thunders.

QUEEN OF LIGHTNING — Thunder Woman

Myth Wife of Big Thunder, Thunder Woman is very beautiful and talented. One day, Thunder Woman was weaving a rainbow-colored blanket when she spied a young and starving boy. She took him in and thus angered her warrior husband. However, with patience and devotion, she persuaded him to accept her truth. She was instrumental in the instruction of the Hailway Chant and participated as the Thunders sang it for Rainboy, as he had unwittingly caused the rift between the Thunders. Another tale of Thunder Woman claims she is married to White Thunder, who is equally quick-tempered and jealous, but White Thunder is much less able to quell his ire, and Thunder Woman is often abandoned by him in his fury.

Symbology Thunder Woman wears a blue dress with a red collar, showing her relationship to sky and to beauty. Sun and Moon are woven into the collar. She holds bullroarers in each wing while medicine pouches dangle from them.

Crooked lightning shoots from both wings and feet and decorates her peaked headdress (common among Shootingway sandpaintings).

Suggested Interpretations A subtle, quick-witted woman who may represent a widow or one unable to have children. She may be in mourning for someone far away. Possibly a woman of sadness. Mourning. Privation. Absence. Loneliness. Separation. One who has savored great happiness but who presently knows the anxiety of misfortune and reversal. Gracefulness, fondness for dancing.

Reversed Narrow-minded. Maliciousness. Bigotry. Deceitfulness. Vengefulness. Prudishness. A treacherous enemy. An ill-tempered person. Gossip.

Guardians A bat and a snake serve as Thunder Woman's guardians, showing her cunning and desire to make peace.

KNIGHT OF LIGHTNING — Blue Thunder Yei

Myth When the first People came to the Fifth World, they had no fire. Part of the time they didn't need it, for it was warm and sunny. Other times, though, it became very cold. One day Hosteen Coyote suggested The People go to Fire Mountain and get a small spark of fire from Thunders who lived there. No one wanted to help him, although two Bird People tried and were scorched for their efforts. Blue Thunder, posing as two Do'tsoh, fire monsters, sent his sparks out to keep all away from the fire. Desperate, Coyote tied a stick to his tail, then went to Blue Thunder Yei and spun a tale of cool water and shifting sands, enticing Blue Thunder to leave his post for moment. The stick caught fire, and though Blue Thunder shot lightning at Coyote, he zigzagged and got away. This is how The People got fire and why the Coyote's tail is still black to this day.

Symbology Blue Thunder Yei wears the red and blue dress of the powerful Thunders. He is armed with bow and arrow to more accurately shoot his magic lightning. Crooked lightning streaks from his unique tipi-styled headdress and rattles dangle from his wings. His entire dress is fringed.

Suggested Interpretations A dashing, brave young man. Though he may be domineering, he has a clean heart. Skill. Capacity. Strength. Heroic action. Opposition and war. Impetuous and fearless rush into the unknown. A master in the art of action and warfare. May mean the coming or going of misfortune.

Reversed Extravagance. Given to bragging. Tyranny over the helpless, be it man or animal. Incapacity. Imprudence. Dispute or ruin over a woman. Impulsive mistakes. Conceited fool. Simplicity.

Guardians None.

PAGE of LightNING
Little Thunder

PAGE OF LIGHTNING — Little Thunder

Myth Big Thunder Yei was very angry at the other Thunders for interfering with his killing of Rainboy. Little Thunder felt sympathy for the young man, torn from life so early. He listened to Bat and to Big Fly when they came to the Thunders to ask for Rainboy's life to be restored. He went to Bat and Big Fly and, in his desire to gain more power, asked if he could serve as one of them, a go-between in the soon-to-be war among the Thunders. And thus, he became the emissary for the Thunders. He can still be heard today, going between the seasons, calling out his tidings.

Symbology Lightning shoots both up and down from Little Thunder's wings, indicating his mid-point position. His dress is red with blue wing-tips. He wears four feathers on his head, three on one side, one dangling down on the other. He also wears a cloud-rattle on his head, showing his sympathy for others.

SUGGESTED INTERPRETATIONS Vigilance. Agility. Spying. A discreet person. An active youth. A lithe figure. A person adept at perceiving, discerning and uncovering the unknown or that which is less than obvious. Dexterity. A message may be coming.

REVERSED An imposter revealed. Illness is possible. Powerlessness in the face of stronger forces. Lack of preparation. Expect the unexpected.

GUARDIANS None.

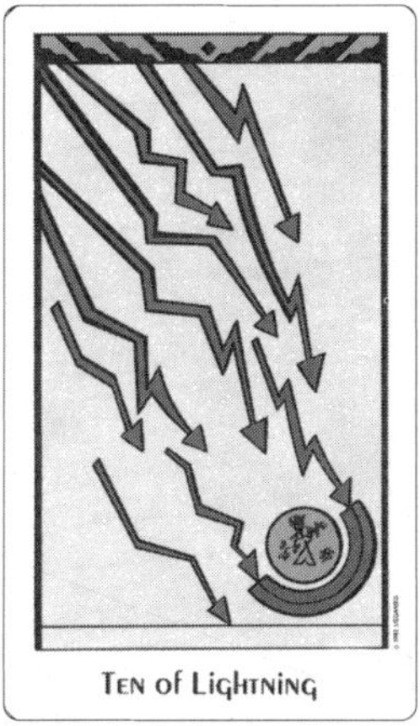

TEN OF LIGHTNING

Symbology Red zigzag lightning bordered in black streak downward in the sky, aiming at the Earth circle which is shown here with a tipi, logs, and sacred plants inside it, representing home, hearth, and the way of life. A curved rainbow rests beneath the Earth circle, but can offer little protection in its position. When reversed, the Earth circle hovers just out of reach of the lightning bolts.

Divinatory Meanings Ruin. Pain. Affliction. Anguish. Desolation. Misfortune. Disappointment. Trouble will come in spite of riches and high position. This is not a card of violent death.

Reversed Benefit. Profit. Temporary gain. Improvement. Passing success. Momentary advantage. Overthrow of evil forces. Courage to rise again.

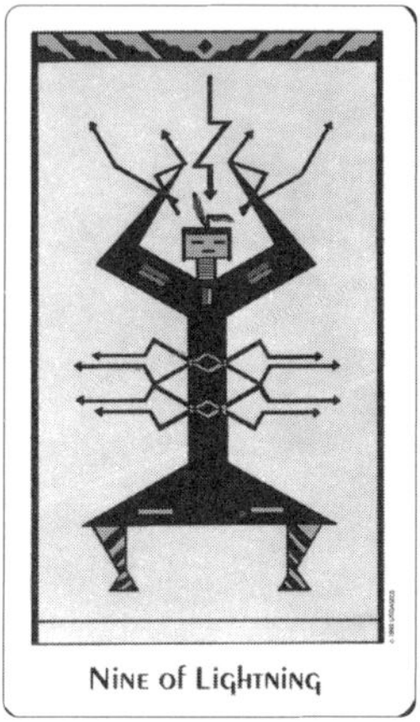

NINE OF LIGHTNING

Symbology A female Yei struggles with uncontrolled crooked lightning. She wears a black dress with minimal decoration. Double-headed crooked lightning crosses her body. One of the nine bolts of lightning is heading downward, straight at her headdress, which is decorated with a single crooked feather. Her leggings are striped. In reversed position, much of that which is uncontrollable about the lightning bolts will simply fade away downward, where it can do little harm.

Divinatory Meanings Concern. Miscarriage. Anxiety over a loved one, possibly the death of someone close. Despair. Loss, doubt.

Reversed Patience, unselfishness. Time brings healing. Tomorrow can be another day. Some doubt may remain.

Eight of Lightning

EIGHT OF LIGHTNING

Symbology A red-dressed young female Yei stands inside the Earth circle, but she is surrounded by eight bolts of lightning. She wears only a single crooked feather as a headdress and carries no medicine pouches or rattles, nothing to aid her escape. In reversed position, she sees she can now simply allow the lightning bolts to pass her by, and fly free.

Divinatory Meanings Narrow or restricted surroundings. Bondage. Crisis. Conflict. Domination. Imprisonment. Turmoil. Bad news. Criticism. Sickness. Calumny. Betrayal. Fear to get out of a bad situation.

Reversed Treachery in the past. Difficulty. Hard work. New beginnings now possible. Impulsive but generous nature. Freedom, but with some doubts.

SEVEN of LIGHTNING

SEVEN OF LIGHTNING

Symbology A male Yei holds five bolts of crooked lightning to one side, protecting them from the smaller bent Yei who now only holds two. Curved rainbow bars hover above and below the bent Yei, offering some consolation. The larger figure wears a warrior headdress and has a rich violet dress. The smaller bent Yei wears the red and blue traditional dress.

Divinatory Meanings A plan that could fail. At the same time, new plans and wishes. Fortitude. Perseverance. Endeavor. Fantasy. A caution against an unwise attempt to make away with what is not yours. Arguments over plans. Partial success.

Reversed Arguments. Uncertain counsel or advice. Possibility of unexpected instruction. Wishes close to being fulfilled.

SIX OF LIGHTNING

Symbology A female Yei assists a Thunder Yei by holding her aloft. The larger figure wears a red dress with an elaborate and dual-feathered headdress and earrings. The smaller Thunder Yei has no headdress but narrow crooked lightning with no spear heads flank her and she stands upon a curved rainbow bar with feathers decorating either side. Six spears of lightning stretch up and outward from both figures. In reverse position, it appears the smaller Yei is being dropped and lightning loses force.

Divinatory Meanings A trip or journey. Headstrong attempts to overcome difficulties. Sending a representative to stand in your stead. Expedient manner. Success after anxiety. Possible new home or journey in consciousness.

Reversed Stalemate. Unwanted proposal. Confession. Declaration. No immediate way out of present difficulties. Unfavorable result of undertaking or lawsuit.

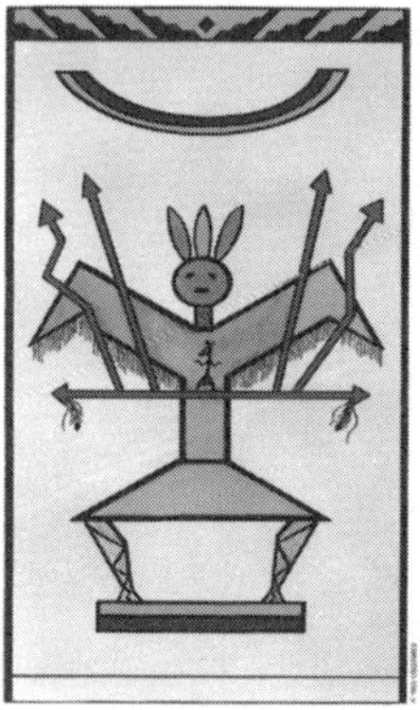

Five of Lightning

FIVE OF LIGHTNING

Symbology A single Thunder Yei stands alone, holding two straight lightning bolts and two crooked lightning bolts upon a large double-headed lightning bolt. He has taken them all and yet did not deserve them. An inverted curved rainbow rests above his three-feathered headdress, as though rejecting him.

Divinatory Meanings Failure, defeat. Conquest by another or destruction of others. Degradation. Adversary may arise. Revocation. Infamy. Dishonor. Unfairness, slander, cruelty.

Reversed Uncertain outlook. Chance of loss or defeat. Weakness. Beware of pride. Possible misfortune befalling a friend. Seduction. Burial. Hollow victory. Sorrow.

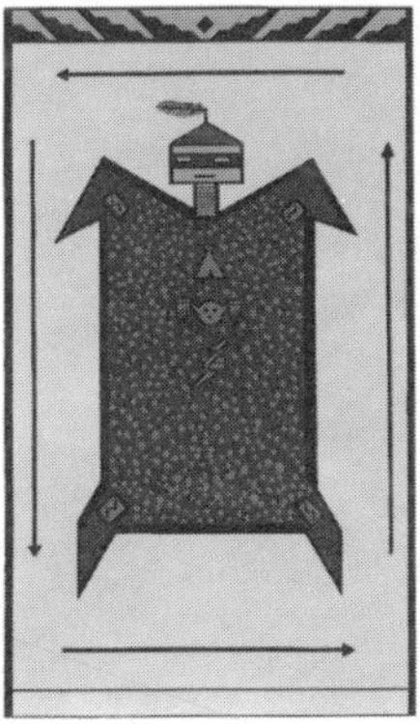

Four of Lightning

FOUR OF LIGHTNING

Symbology A Shootingway headdressed female Thunder Yei is dressed in black with the constellations decorating her dress. Also inside her dress are a tipi, a moon, logs, and four single-barred rainbows. Four bolts of straight lightning surround her, one above, one below, and two flanking her. They travel clockwise in the same motion as the Earth rotates.

Divinatory Meanings Respite. Rest after illness. Repose. Replenishment. Solitude. Exile. Retreat. Relaxation of anxiety, release from suffering. Abandonment.

Reversed Renewed activity. A caution to be circumspect. Qualified success. Guarded advancement. Desire to recover what is lost.

THREE OF LIGHTNING

Symbology Two male bent Yeis, reverses of each other, stand on either side of a large bolt of crooked lightning. Both hold a single bolt of crooked lightning in one hand. Each wear a three-feathered headdress and wear the round eyes and mouth of the warrior or the ghost figures. Even in reverse position, these two Yeis are separated, troubled.

Divinatory Meanings Absence. Sorrow. Disappointment. Strife. Removal. Dispersion. Diversion. Opposition. Separation. Delay.

Reversed Distraction. Confusion. Disorder. Error. Mistake. Incompatibility. Anxiety. Loss. Alienation.

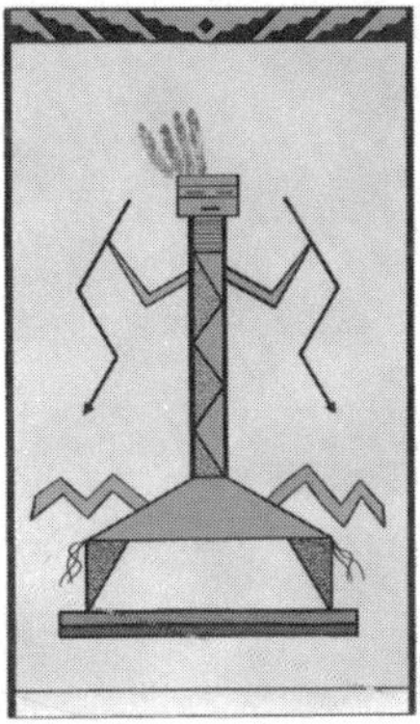

Two of Lightning

TWO OF LIGHTNING

Symbology Mountains in the far distance almost appear an extension of this Thunder Yei's skirt. She wears three feathers as her headdress. She carries a crooked lightning bolt in each hand, but the speared heads point downward. She stands upon a rainbow bar.

Divinatory Meanings Tension in relationships. Indecision. Military friendships. Balanced forces at work. Harmony in some areas, though not those close to you. Firmness. Concord. Offsetting factors. Stalemate.

Reversed Duplicity. Misrepresentation. Dishonor. Treachery. False friends. Lies. Could have sympathy for those in trouble.

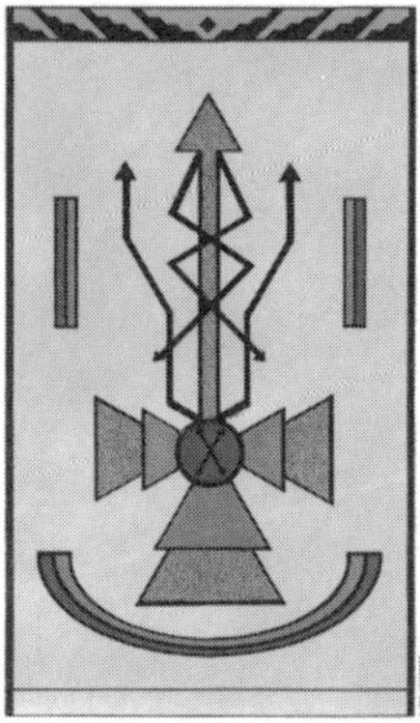

Ace of Lightning

ACE OF LIGHTNING

Symbology A single, large, straight lightning bolt shoots skyward, criss-crossed by narrow bolts of lightning going downward and two crooked lightning bolts streaking upward. The central lightning bolt extends from the Earth circle which has decorative cloud towers emanating to the right and left of the Earth and one stretching beneath. A curved rainbow bar rests beneath the central lightning bolt while two smaller straight rainbow bars flank it.

Divinatory Meanings Conquest. Great determination. Initiative. Strength. Force. Activity. Excessiveness. Triumph. Power. Success. Fertility. Prosperity. Deep emotional feeling, either love or hate. Championship. Possible birth of a warrior child.

Reversed Debacle. Tyranny. Disaster. Self-destruction. Violent temper. Embarrassment. Obstacle. Infertility. Disastrous victory.

SUIT OF BUFFALO

When Monster Slayer and First Born returned from their travels and visiting the home of their father, The Sun, Monster Slayer began talking about an amazing sight he had seen in the opening his father had made. He told The People he saw an abundance of game roaming all over the place. They were in the South, in the West, and in the North also. And before the game was another wonderful sight; an enormous amount of jewels were spread out. He talked with The People and all decided he should go to this wonderful place. When he got there, he would see various animals, only to approach them and find they had turned into plants. He was very discouraged and disappointed. Finally, he discovered that by following the plants, he could find the animals, and that is when he met the Buffalo People.

The Buffalo People are rich and follow trails of water to find those things that enrich their lives. Known as the Ay-yah-neh, the Buffalo People are known for their astute trading, their careful accumulation of riches, and their ceremonial knowledge passed down from generation to generation. Because they are largely nomadic in nature, their garnering of riches is very particular, as the Buffalo People must carry what they acquire. Therefore, much of what they consider wealth is more symbolic than real.

The Buffalo People are a taciturn group, keeping secrets easily and dedicated to hard work and the rewards gained from the work. They are associated with plants, animals, and learning.

The Buffalo suit in The Santa Fe Tarot Deck corresponds to the suit of Pentacles or Coins and is usually selected for people with black hair and dark eyes. The element is earth and the direction, east. This is the suit of money, fortune, and trade.

The border of the Buffalo suit is dark green and the four court cards of the suit are also represented against this darker green background. The ten suit cards are drawn against a paler green background. The design at the top of the Buffalo cards are taken from the central pattern of a Teec Nos Pos Navajo rug in the Four Corners region of the United States.

Far, far away from Buffalo Country
Hither now they come with their little ones,
Rapidly now they walk, rapidly they walk,
Even now they walk, rapidly they walk,
Even now they reach the Red Bird Cap.

O Buffalo Old Man, O Buffalo Old Woman!
Come hither rapidly with your little ones.
Navajo

KING OF BUFFALO — Big Buffalo Yei

Myth One day the Chief of the Ay-yah-neh, the Buffalo People, discovered a man had taken the Chief's daughter to wed. He was saddened by this marriage for he didn't believe the young man to be worthy of his daughter. Soon it was time for the Buffalo People to return to their home on the Plains of the East, and he approached the young man and told him not to follow them. The young man did not heed him, and when he was discovered, Big Buffalo Yei resolved to kill the young man. However, the young man had special magic he'd received from the gods and killed the Buffalo People instead. When the young man saw what he had done, he was filled with remorse and revived Big Buffalo Yei for a conference. Big Buffalo Yei told the young man he would confer very special ceremonial knowledge upon him in exchange for restoring the rest of his People. The young man agreed to this bargain and did as Big Buffalo Yei requested. Big Buffalo Yei also kept his part of the agreement. He never saw the young man again, but

The People know this is how they acquired the knowledge of calling animals to them.

Symbology Big Buffalo Yei is represented here with his Buffalo body and Yei head. Inside his body is a sacred plant and a painted white hand symbol. His headdress is the peaked hat commonly found in the Shootingway, part of the Sun Group ceremonies. The peak is adorned with feathers as is his sash. In his hands he carries Earth circles, two smaller circles linked by a single trail of blue water, and the larger supported by a modified cloud rattle.

Suggested Interpretations An experienced and successful leader. A person of character and intelligence. Business acumen. Mathematical ability. Loyal friend. Reliable marriage partner. Wise investment. Ability to acquire money and valuable possessions.

Reversed Corruption. Using any means to achieve the desired end. Vice. Avarice. Unfaithfulness. An old and vicious man. Peril. Thriftless. Perverse use of talents.

Guardians Big Buffalo Yei is protected at upper right and lower left of this painting by bat guardians.

QUEEN OF BUFFALO — Buffalo Woman

Myth Buffalo Woman is the daughter of Big Buffalo Yei, the girl who married outside of her People. She was saddened when her husband killed her People, and glad when he revived them for their knowledge. However, after he left them, she found she was to have a baby. While this might have made any other woman sad, Buffalo Woman was happy in her motherhood. She spent many hours preparing fine things for the child, for Bat had come to Buffalo Woman and told her that the child would be special to her People. She fashioned a beautiful cradleboard for the child and decorated it with the four sacred plants for bounty, a butterfly for beauty, and Earth circles for riches. When the baby was born he rode in the cradleboard and all who saw him recognized him as a Great One. And whenever The People see him now, or see his mother, Buffalo Woman, all know that good luck will come their way.

Symbology Buffalo Woman is shown here as part Buffalo and part Yei. She wears the peaked hat and feathered headdress of those Yeis found in the Shootingway Chant, which shows her strength and indomitability. Inside her body she has the weasel prong, showing her cunning and compassion. An inverted moon is also painted on her dress, as is the sacred bean plant. She holds an Earth circle in the palm of one hand and carries another from a trail of blue water. Below her, a blue crooked snake travels North. A curved rainbow bar hovers behind her and a big butterfly adorns the lower right of the sandpainting.

Suggested Interpretations Prosperity and well-being. Abundance. Opulence. Extreme comfort. Generosity. Security. Liberty. Magnificence. Grace. Dignity. A rich person but generous and charitable. A noble soul. At times moody and melancholy. Can often be a kind widow.

Reversed False prosperity. Suspense. Suspicion. Responsibilities neglected. Distrustful person. Fear of failure. Dependence on others.

Guardians Double tipis in the lower left and upper right corners of the sandpainting show that while she may travel from place to place, she always makes a home wherever she is.

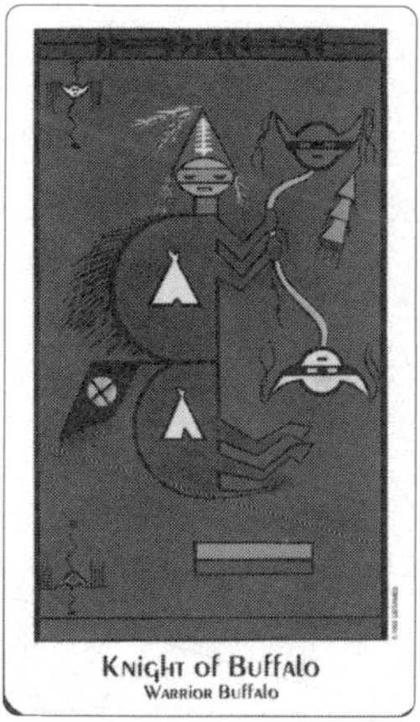

KNIGHT OF BUFFALO — Warrior Buffalo

Myth When the Chief of the Buffalo People made peace with others, there was one who wasn't happy with this peace. He was called Warrior Buffalo. He had seen many Buffalo People die and he wanted revenge upon their killers. He didn't listen to the peace words, but heard instead the songs and ceremonies of those who had fought before. He knew that in order to be strong he had to do a lot of running, so he ran at morning, at noon, and in the evening. And he knew that to be strong, he had to jump in the cold, cold water. This he did as well. Finally, when he was strong enough, he gathered other like-minded young warriors and they set forth to battle their enemies. They made camp and sang the Enemyway. They called upon Monster Slayer to protect them. And in the morning they made a battle with the others they found on the banks of a river. Many were killed on both sides and many tchindi (bad spirits) were released and haunted the living. It took many ceremonies to cleanse Warrior Buffalo from the bad spirits. But from those days forward, Warrior Buffalo knew that killing wasn't the only way a warrior can prove his strength.

Symbology Warrior Buffalo is depicted here with a maroon-brown body holding tipis inside, showing his desire to protect his home. He carries an orange water trail with a warrior-marked inverted sun and upright masked moon. From one of the Moon's horns dangles a decorated bullroarer. In one hand Warrior Buffalo carries a string he has knotted to mark the days before going to war. Warrior Buffalo's peaked hat is marked with bones and decorated with feathers. His sash has an Earth circle drawn upon it. A rainbow bar supports him.

Suggested Interpretations A mature and responsible person. Reliable. Methodical. Patient. Persistent ability to conclude a task. Laborious. Organized. A person who has learned the lessons of the past and has put them to good use.

Reversed Stagnation. Inertia. Lack of determination or direction. Narrow-mindedness. Carelessness. Limits set by dogmatic views. Idleness.

Guardians Sun and Moon guardians protect Warrior Buffalo from the upper and lower left of the sandpainting in non-traditional position.

PAGE OF BUFFALO — Buffalo Child

Myth One day a child was born to the Ay-yah-nch, and the Buffalo People knew him immediately to be a special youth. He soon outgrew his cradleboard and was ready for traveling. And this the Buffalo People knew he had been born to do. He set out to learn all he could from the Magic People, the Hash-Tye Din'neh, the Yeis who held all the knowledge of the sacred ceremonies. He met with Calling God, Black God, Sun, Moon, Big Star, the Thunder People, the Rainbow People, and over time, even the Deer and Antelope People. Because of his great desire to learn, The People helped him in his quest. The Yeis formed a magic string and knotted it for each of the new ceremonies Buffalo Child mastered. He was told to carry this at all times for it would let everyone know of his status as ha'atathli.

Symbology Though Buffalo Child is referred to by male gender, he wears a female Yei face, showing his mutability.

His peaked hat is blue and decorated with dyed turquoise feathers. He wears jeweled earrings given him by one of his many teachers. In one hand he carries a stylized tipi, in the other his knotted string of ceremonial knowledge. His body is double-sided, indicating his steadfastness. An Earth circle hovers beneath his knotted string and above an inverted Sun. Buffalo Child stands upon the flat plain beside a huge mountain range.

Suggested Interpretations Deep concentration and application. Scholarship. Reflection. Desire for new ideas. A do-gooder. Bearer of news. Good management, carefulness. Can mean messages about money.

Reversed An unrealistic person. Failure to recognize obvious facts. Dissipation of ideas. Illogical thinking. Rebelliousness. Wastefulness. Unfavorable news.

Guardians Bat and The Sun serve as Buffalo Child's eastern guardians, sealing the upper left and right corners of this painting.

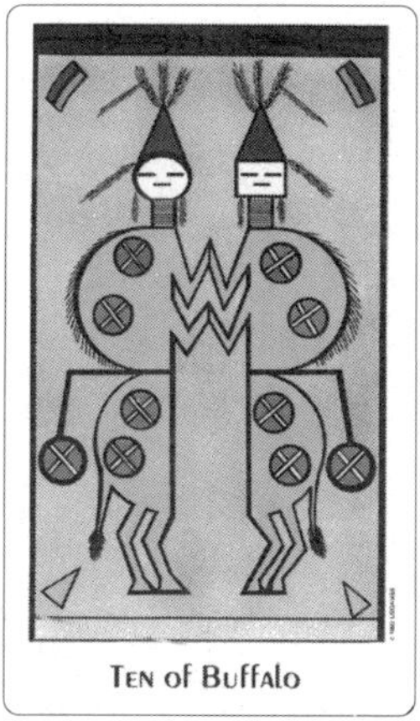

TEN OF BUFFALO

Symbology A male and female Buffalo Yei face each other and touch hands. Their bodies each contain four Earth circles and the sash of each dress is made up of another, making ten circles in all. Tipis point toward them in the lower corners of the painting while curved rainbow bars serve as the guardians.

Divinatory Meanings Riches. Safety. Attention to family matters. Ancestry. Inheritance. The acquisition of a home. Security.

Reversed Bad odds. Possible loss. Hazard. Robbery. Loss of inheritance. Dissipation. Gambling. Risky proposition.

Nine of Buffalo

NINE OF BUFFALO

Symbology A solitary Buffalo figure stands upon the last hill of a mountain range. His horns curve upward while a weasel prong serves as his down-turned mouth. Two Earth circles are seen in his body while two lie within the mountains and another is perched on the very pinnacle of the tallest peak. Four green Earth circles rest in each corner of the painting. His position here reflects his solitary state, yet the many Earth circles show his abundance of riches.

Divinatory Meanings Solitary enjoyment of the good things of life. Accomplishment. Discernment. Discretion. Foresight. Prudence. Material well-being. Love of nature and gardening.

Reversed Roguery. Danger. Storms. Bad faith. Possible loss of a valued friendship or a treasured possession.

Eight of Buffalo

EIGHT OF BUFFALO

Symbology Two Buffalo People, a male and a female, dovetail each other, each holding an Earth circle in the palms of their outstretched hands and two more within their bodies. Each wears a single feather as a headdress and both have decorated earrings. Two black and white Earth circles hover in the sky, one just out of reach, the other behind the Buffalo People. In all four corners, Sun and Moon guardians with knotted-string decorations protect the sandpainting.

Divinatory Meanings Apprenticeship. Craftsmanship. Quickness to learn. Candor. Modesty. Handiwork. Personal effort. The beginning of a profitable undertaking. Employment or commission to come.

Reversed Lack of ambition. Vanity. Conceit. Disillusionment. Usury. Hypocrisy. Flattery. Intrigue. Skill turned to cunning.

Seven of Buffalo

SEVEN OF BUFFALO

Symbology A Buffalo is suspended above a mountain range, neither reaching nor acquiring the five colored Earth circles or the two black and white circles inside the mountain. The Earth circles within the mountain range are attached by a sacred bean plant, and the ones upon the mountain peaks are decorated with strings that contain no knots. The buffalo figure has a weasel-pronged mouth and a black hand on his rump.

Divinatory Meanings A pause during the development of an enterprise. Unprofitable speculations. Anxiety about a loan. Ingenuity. Growth. Hard work. Progress may be attained, but slowly.

Reversed Impatience. Uneasiness. Imprudent actions. Loss of money. Unwise investments. Little gain after much work.

SIX OF BUFFALO

Symbology A Buffalo Yei travels in the mountains carrying two earth-colored Earth circles in each hand and wearing a white deerskin decorated with sacred plants. He wears a red peaked hat with three feathers and rattles on his feet. Before him are four black tipis with Earth circles instead of doorways. A curved rainbow bar protects his passage through the mountains.

Divinatory Meanings Generosity. Philanthropy. Charity. Kindness. Gratification. Gifts. Material gain. Things received which are deserved.

Reversed Avarice. Selfishness. Envy. Jealousy. Bad debt. Gifts given, but as a bribe. Present prosperity threatened.

Five of Buffalo

FIVE OF BUFFALO

Symbology A male Buffalo Yei stands empty-handed, palms upward, as if trying to reach the five decorated tipis with Earth circle doorways. All feathers on the tipis face away from him. He wears a connected Sun-Moon guardian pair in his blouse and a black hand on his withers.

Divinatory Meanings Unemployment. Destitution. Loss. Failure. Error. Mistress. Lovers unable to find a meeting place. Loneliness. Affinities may be found, but through similar troubles.

Reversed Reversal of bad trend. New interest in spiritual matters. Overcoming ruin. Disharmony in marriage or love interests. New employment, but may not be permanent. Charity offered or taken.

Four of Buffalo

FOUR OF BUFFALO

Symbology Four Buffalo People rotate clockwise around four Earth circles resting on a modified Whirling Logs cross. The Buffalo People are earth-toned, blue, red, and black, and each wears that color's feathers and has a weasel-pronged mouth. The feeling is one of movement and progress. Each of the Buffalo People shown here are drawn in running motion.

Divinatory Meanings Assured material gain. Earthly power, but can lead to love of material wealth, not spiritual. Can indicate inheritance or gifts, but caution should be taken not to become a hoarder. Usurer. Skinflint. Inability to share.

Reversed Setbacks in material matters. Opposition to further gain. Prejudice, covetousness. Suspense and delay. Spendthrift.

Three of Buffalo

THREE OF BUFFALO

Symbology A Buffalo figure with lighter colored horns, a white hand and a weasel-pronged mouth runs between three large Earth circles with Zia or Sun lines radiating out from each. As is common with Earth circles, the four divided sections indicate the four elements, four seasons, four walks of life, and four components of a happy home: food, fire, water, and tipi.

Divinatory Meanings Great skill in trade or work. Mastery. Perfection. Artistic ability. Dignity. Renown. Rank. Power. Indicates gain in commercial transaction.

Reversed Sloppiness. Mediocrity. Money problems. Commonplace ideas or goals. Lack of skill. Preoccupation with material gain.

Two of Buffalo

TWO OF BUFFALO

Symbology Two Buffalo figures seemingly toss the red Earth circles in their hooves. The Earth circles are joined by blue water trails, some touching, others not. Eight tipis with small circles for doorways surround the two Buffalo figures. The two lower tipis are adorned with feathers.

Divinatory Meanings The ability to juggle more than one situation at a time. Lightheartedness. Gaiety. Difficulty in launching new projects. Difficult situations. New troubles. Embarrassment. Changeable moods; elated, then melancholic.

Reversed Literary ability. Lack of agility in handling matters. Simulated enjoyment. Enforced gaiety. Letter. Message.

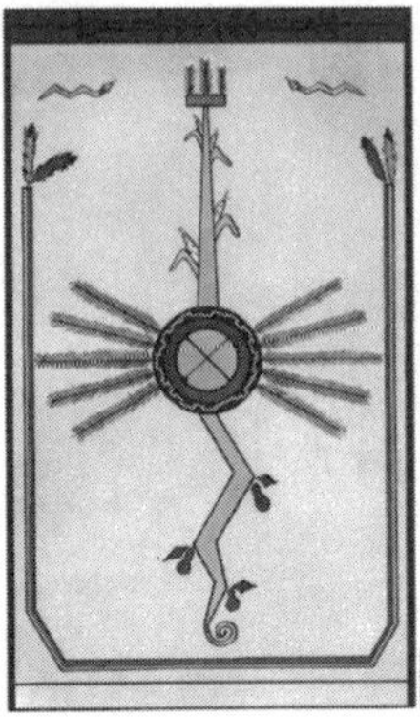

Ace of Buffalo

ACE OF BUFFALO

Symbology An Earth circle rests in the center of a Sun-like arrangement of sacred plants: bean, corn, squash, and tobacco. The plants are at full harvest, each ready to pick. The green circle around the Earth circle indicates water and growth, while the patterned black circle shows the rituals and ceremonies necessary for abundance. The plants and circles are protected by a feather-decorated rainbow border and further made secure by two crooked snake guardians.

Divinatory Meanings Perfection. Attainment. Prosperity. Felicity. Bliss. Gold. Valuable coins or artifacts. Treasures. The combination of material and spiritual riches. Pleasure and beauty are present.

Reversed Prosperity without happiness. Misused wealth. Wasted money. Corruption by money. Miserliness. Greed. Fool's gold. False start.

5

How To Read The Santa Fe Tarot Deck

The first step to reading or divining any Tarot cards is familiarizing yourself with the symbology of the deck. Study the imagery on each card; see it not so much with your eyes as with your heart and your spirit. Allow the Holy Ones to speak through the various Yeis and figures presented in The Santa Fe Tarot deck and listen to their messages and instruction.

Each reader/diviner has his or her own unique method of preserving the vibrations of the cards, and how you choose to go about it will prove your own unique way. Some believe that wrapping the cards in a silk scarf in between each usage will not only keep the cards from physical damage but maintain their mystical integrity. Others believe that sleeping with them beneath their pillow allows their own personal vibrations to enter and mingle with the cards.

As these cards reflect Navajo religion and myth, it is possible that you will choose to handle the book and cards much as a Navajo ha'atathli or medicine man might do. A ha'atathli always keeps his medicine pouch or bundle near him and will touch it and talk over it at least daily, even when not performing a ceremony. Before performing a healing, the ha'atathli usually will lay his or her hands upon the precious medicine bundle or pouch and say a quiet prayer to the Holy Ones. This is said to open the mind to the messages and healing powers the supernaturals govern, and allows the medicine man to transfer those powers to the patient (the querent in this case).

The suggested layouts of The Santa Fe Tarot Deck are derived by adapting one of the most popular and effective methods of using the tarot for divination—the ten-card spread—and four of the ceremonial Ways known to the Navajo. In this way, the reader/diviner can discover the properties of the lengthy and complex Navajo methods used to restore balance, and employ a variation of Arthur Edward Waite's Ancient Celtic Method, as seen in *The Pictorial Key to the Tarot.*

In Navajo belief, restoration of balance is the key to a happy life and a future filled with harmony. In order to restore balance to a seeker, it is often necessary to enlist the aid of a ha'atathli, or spiritual leader. The reader/diviner, while using The Santa Fe Tarot Deck, serves in the guise of ha'atathli.

The diviner sits with the questioner, or querent, usually opposite each other, either at a table or upon the floor. As restoration of balance is of paramount importance, both parties should approach all the Ways with serious intent.

The methods presented in this book are designed for slightly different questions. For example, the Navajo Windway chant primarily focuses upon the hero/heroine's experience of and extrication from a specific predicament. Therefore, the Windway would be of greater assistance in answering a particular question or a general overview of a particular matter. On the other hand, The Blessingway, which relates to general harmony or disharmony in life, would better serve a broad, non-specific reading.

Some of the methods described in the following sections require the diviner and questioner to first select a card to represent the questioner. In the traditional Celtic Cross method (included), the card used to represent the questioner is taken from one of the suit Court cards: King, Queen, Knight, or Page.

In The Santa Fe Tarot Deck, dark-haired, dark-eyed persons are represented by the suits of Water and Buffalo, while lighter-haired, paler-eyed persons can be represented by the suits of Rainbows and Lightning. A King generally relates to a married or older man, the Queen to a married or adult woman, the Knight to a young or unmarried man, and the Page to either a male or female who is youthful in both appearance and attitude.

If the method selected calls for such a card, upon selection it is placed in a central position, usually facing the diviner or ha'atathli. At this point, the questioner carefully considers what he or she wishes to learn. This question may be stated aloud to the diviner while the questioner shuffles the face-down deck, or can be silently pondered as the diviner does so.

Many Tarot diviners believe the person who handles the cards impregnates them with personal magnetism and thereby creates a rapport between the subconscious and the cards. They prefer, therefore, that the questioner shuffle the cards. Others, believing that the cards maintain a purity of rapport between diviner and message, prefer to personally shuffle the cards, only allowing the questioner to cut the deck while mindful of the question posed. The consideration of who shuffles the cards and who cuts them should be determined at the discretion of the diviner or ha'atathli.

Before turning to a specific method or Way, some important details of Tarot interpretation should be taken into account.

- The cards should be turned over from the narrow edges of the card from left to right and not interpreted until all the cards have been laid out.

- The cards with pictures upside down to the diviner are said to be reversed and therefore the reverse meanings supplied in the book and booklet apply to them. Generally, if more than half the cards are reversed, the diviner may find a better reading is obtained by moving the reversed cards to upright position.

- The cards should be studied and analyzed thoroughly before beginning an interpretation. This allows the diviner to see the broader picture before attempting to provide a reading.

After studying the cards, and before verbal interpretation, mentally arrange them into categories: Major Arcana, Rainbows, Water, Lightning, and Buffalo. More of one suit than another gives insight into the reader's question. As a general trend, this simple formula can aid in a reading:

3 – 4 (or more)	**Major Arcana** Outside influences at work
3 – 4 (or more)	**Rainbows** Change or growth
3 – 4 (or more)	**Water** Love, goodness
3 – 4 (or more)	**Lightning** Strife
3 – 4 (or more)	**Buffalo** Political action, intrigue

Readings depend on the complete picture, how cards might relate to each other, and to which position they were placed in the overall layout. For example, the Death card appearing in a 'distant past' location would have an entirely different interpretation than if it were located in a 'final outcome' location. The first might mean that a great change took place in the querent's past, while the latter could indicate the coming of a transformation in his or her life.

While each card in the Santa Fe Tarot book is presented with suggested interpretative meanings and reversed meanings, these are intended as general guidance only. Over time, and with careful study of the Navajo symbology, the reader should be able to rely upon his/her own sense of intuition and understanding of the symbology to 'see' a deeper picture, a broader spectrum of implication of the powers that rule the Universe.

The reading of the cards is a great responsibility and should never be done with negativity in mind. As a general rule, whatever layout is used, **never** end a reading on a negative note. Even should every card in a reading hold difficult problems to resolve (which is nearly impossible), these still are only insights to growth and spiritual development. It would be wise to recall that a life without strife, a love without problems, a home without some difficulty all indicate an existence without soul.

In beauty may I walk.
Soft goods may I acquire.
Hard goods may I acquire.
Horses may I acquire.
Sheep may I acquire.
In old age wandering.
Trail beautiful.
Lively may I walk.
NAVAJO

The Windway Spread

The Navajo Windway myth is characterized by the plot pattern of instruction of the hero by predicament and extrication. This is a common theme among the various Ways of the Navajo, because it is believed that knowledge can best be learned by experience, and wisdom gained by pitting one's self against the mysterious, powerful forces in the universe.

The Windway Spread allows the questioner to either seek an answer to a specific question or to ask for a general overview of a specific or particular event or problem in life. Upon deciding to use The Windway, the diviner and the questioner must first agree upon a card to represent the questioner. For guidance in selecting this card, see page 147.

Once the questioner's card has been selected, it is placed in a central position, usually facing the diviner or ha'atathli. At this point, the questioner carefully considers what he or she wishes to learn. This question may be stated aloud to the diviner while the questioner shuffles the face down deck, or can be silently pondered as the diviner does so.

Beginning with the questioner's designated card as number one, and traveling counter-clockwise, the second card turned over is called number two, and so on. The diviner turns over the first five cards, one at a time, placing them face up on the table in the sequence shown in the diagram.

The cards with pictures upside down to the diviner are said to be reversed and therefore the reverse meanings apply to them. Generally, if more than half the cards are reversed, the diviner may find a better reading is obtained by moving the reversed cards to upright position.

The Windway spread adapts the ancient Celtic Method with the Navajo Windway. Its motion is counter clockwise, and its number is 10.

The Windway Spread

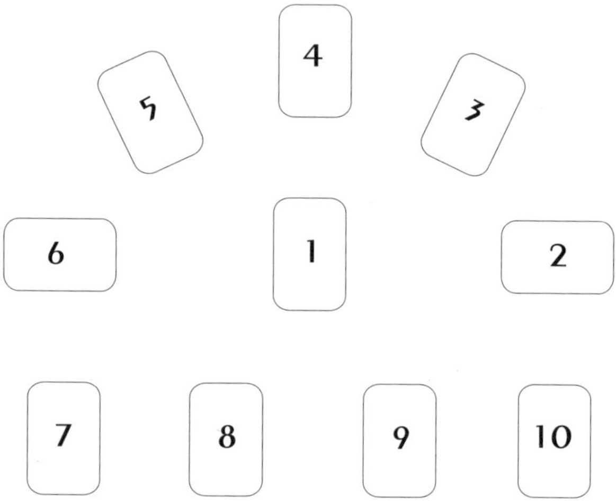

1. The Questioner.
2. Immediate Influence.
3. Goal or Destiny.
4. Distant Past Foundation.
5. Recent Past Events.
6. Future Influence.
7. The Self.
8. Life.
9. Inner Emotions.
10. Final Results.

The significance of the cards in the Windway Spread is as follows:

Card 1 The Questioner. Attributes of the card represent the questioner and the point from which the questioner is presently working and living.

Card 2 Immediate Influence. The nature of the influences or the obstacles that lie just ahead. This card faces the questioner.

Card 3 Goal or Destiny. The ultimate goal or destiny of the questioner. The best that can be accomplished by the questioner based on existing circumstances. This card may also represent the questioner's aim or ideal within the present frame of reference. This card flanks the questioner.

Card 4 Distant Past Foundation. The broad and basic events and influences which existed in the past and upon which the present events are based. This card rests upon the questioner.

Card 5 Recent Past Events. The most recent sphere of influence or events that has passed or is just passing. The card may represent distant past influences exerting pressure on recent events. This card also flanks the questioner.

Card 6 Future Influence. In a broad sense, this is the sphere of influence that is coming into being in the near future. This card beckons the questioner.

After reading the preceding five cards around the questioner card, the diviner proceeds to turn over the next four cards from the deck, placing them one after another in a line below the previous six cards, as in the diagram.

Card 7 The Self. The questioner's present position or attitude within the circumstances. This card is used to place the questioner in proper perspective.

Card 8 Life. The questioner's influence on other people and his or her position in life. Tendencies and factors that exist with respect to other persons who may have an effect on the questioner.

Card 9 Inner Emotions. The inner hopes, hidden emotions and secret desires, fears and anxieties of the questioner. Includes those thoughts which will come to the mind of the questioner in the future.

Card 10 Final Results. The culmination of all the influences revealed by the other cards in the divination, provided events and influences continue as indicated.

The Nightway Spread

The Navajo Nightway is a nine-night extended ceremonial. In the Nightway, a dreamer or visionary travels extensively, seeking guidance from the gods and learning from them many magical things. Like the Windway, the Nightway is episodic and deals with the hero learning from a number of experiences. The Nightway, however, focuses less on the external self than on the inner self, the self that could be.

The Nightway Spread is offers a complete method of laying out the cards when the querent is seeking an answer to questions related to dreams, aspirations, goals, or fears.

Select a card to represent the querent. See page 147 for guidelines to the selection of this card.

At this point, the representative card can either be set aside or re-shuffled into the deck. If it is re-shuffled into the deck, and should appear as one of the 10 cards in the Nightway Spread, special attention should be paid to the meaning of the number at which location it appeared. For example, should the querent's representative card be the Queen of Rainbows—Rainbow Woman—and it appears after shuffling and cutting at the 'nine' position, governing intelligence, science, crafts, and procreation, any of these things might be of particular significance or be of special interest to the querent in a quest for spiritual knowledge.

The diviner shuffles the deck and has the querent cut the cards three times, left to right, while carefully considering a question. The cards are then laid out as shown in the diagram, in three tiers, a trunk, and a spire. If a straight line is drawn up the center from the one to the four to the seven and, finally, the ten, and curved lines radiating out from each of the central numbers, one can easily see a corn plant in full bounty.

All cards are turned over from left to right and studied carefully. The tiers of the corn plant should be interpreted separately, then as a whole. As a general rule, the first tier represents spirituality or highest ideals; the second tier relates to the intellectual and moral nature of the querent; and the third tier reflects the querent's ability to direct and control his or her destiny. The tenth card, the final outcome card, relates to the querent's material world—the home, the body.

The Nightway Spread

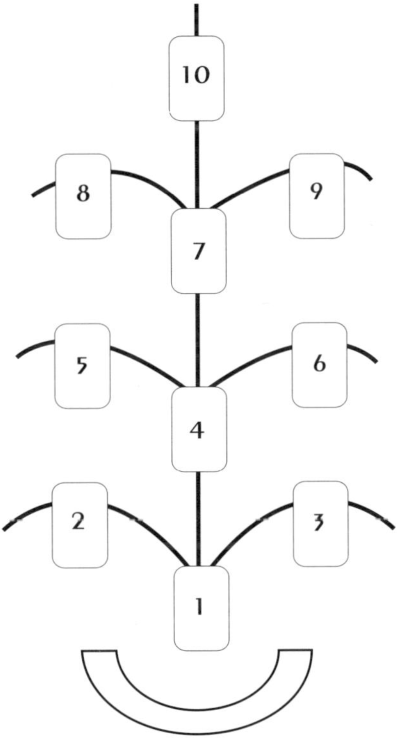

1. The Seeker's Highest Ideals.
2. The Seeker's Creativity.
3. The Seeker's Wisdom.
4. The Seeker's Virtues.
5. The Seeker's Vulnerabilities.
6. The Seeker's Actions.
7. The Seeker's Love, lust and Creative Instincts.
8. The Seeker's Actions.
9. The Seeker's Imagination.
10. The Final Outcome.

When a pattern has emerged, the cards should be interpreted in the order indicated. The significance of the placement is as follows:

Card 1 The Seeker's Highest Ideals. This card represents that which the seeker most deeply believes should be.

Card 2 The Seeker's Innate Creativity. This card reflects the gifts the seeker has been born with, whether used or not.

Card 3 The Seeker's Wisdom. This is the reflection of what the seeker has, from experience, brought into his or her life. Generally equated with what the seeker has done with his or her innate gifts.

Card 4 The Seeker's Virtues, Qualities, and Abilities. This card reflects skills, knowledge, certainties.

Card 5 The Seeker's Vulnerabilities. This card indicates those areas where the seeker may need strength or caution.

Card 6 The Seeker's Actions. This card expresses the seeker's dealings with others and can reflect the depth to which a person will become involved in another's life.

Card 7 The Seeker's Love, Lust, and Creative Instincts. This card reflects the seeker's innermost feelings.

Card 8 The Seeker's Ambitions. This card reveals the querent's overt goals in life and the manner in which he or she has striven to accomplish these goals.

Card 9 The Seeker's Imagination. This card indicates the querent's psychic abilities, intuitive nature, and responsiveness to spiritual matters.

Card 10 The Final Outcome. This card should be considered only after all other cards have been studied and read. Its meaning only reflects the culmination of the messages revealed by all preceding cards. It reflects what 'should be' about to happen in the seeker's life, in light of what the seeker has contributed.

(If the querent's card has been set aside to use with the reading, it is now read with the meaning of the card to better reflect the final outcome card.)

The Blessingway Spread

Although a separate ceremonial chant, the Blessingway rite is said to control all the chantways. One ha'atathli, Long Mustache, called the Blessingway the spinal column of all songs. Even the Enemyway rite closes by singing the twelve-word Blessingway song.

The actual Navajo word for Blessingway, hoh'zho-oh-li, stems from a word which has no direct translation into English. By overall concept, it can be said that the word relates to everything a Navajo considers good: beauty, perfection, harmony, normality, success, well-being, order, and that which is favorable to The People.

The Blessingway ceremonial is used for many reasons, from rite of passage into puberty, to childbirth, to weddings. No matter what the specific might be, however, the aim is to create good hope and good luck; avert misfortune; and obtain the blessings needed for a long, happy life.

The Blessingway Spread should be used when a non-specific, general view of the querent's life is requested. Its movement is clockwise and circular, and its number is nine. No representative card is needed for the querent, though should one of the Court cards which closely resembles the seeker appear in the reading, it should be given greater significance than it might otherwise hold.

The diviner shuffles the cards and the seeker cuts them nine times. The diviner then lays out the nine cards in a circular shape (as shown in the Blessingway diagram) leaving an Eastern entrance at the top of the layout, much as a sandpainting would do. The cards are turned over left to right and placed in a clockwise direction.

The Blessingway Spread

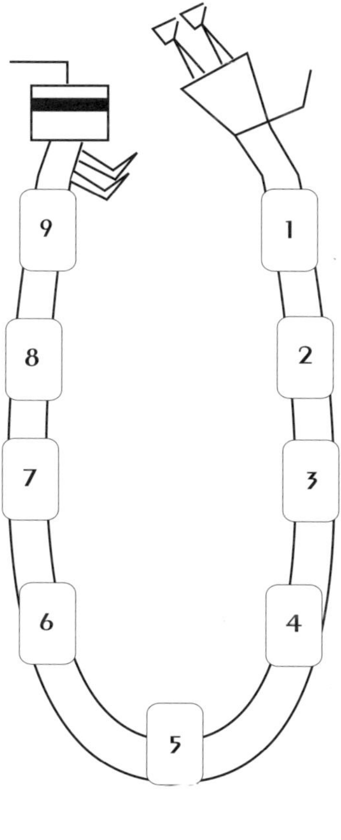

1. Distant Past.
2. Recent Past.
3. Current State of Affairs.
4. The Seeker's Impact on Others.
5. Other's Impact on Seeker.
6. The Seeker's Inner Dreams.
7. The Seeker's Inner Fears.
8. The Future Influence.
9. The Final Outcome.

The significance of the Blessingway Spread is as follows:

Card 1 Distant Past. This card reflects the seeker's distant past.

Card 2 Recent Past. This card indicates those things which have only just happened in the querent's life.

Card 3 Current State of Affairs. This reflects the seeker's present position in life.

Card 4 The Seeker's Impact on Others. This card indicates how the seeker has influenced or affected others around him or her.

Card 5 Other's Impact on the Seeker. This card reflects the manner in which others have impacted the seeker's life.

Card 6 The Seeker's Inner Dreams. This card reveals the seeker's secret hopes in relation to happiness in life.

Card 7 The Seeker's Inner Fears. This card reveals the seeker's innermost fear in relation to attainment of goals.

Card 8 The Future Influence. This card shows the nature of influences or obstacles that affect the final outcome.

Card 9 The Final Outcome. This card reflects the culmination of all the influences revealed by the other cards in the reading, provided that which has been indicated continues.

The Hailway Spread

A lengthy ceremonial, involving many sandpaintings and several days and nights of singing, the Hailway Chant is now considered extinct. The last man said to know it, Hosteen Klah, is believed to have died being the only one with the full knowledge of its preparation. What is known of the chant is that it was used to avert both large and small disasters relating to thunder, lightning, rain, and hail. (Larger disasters would include such things as cyclones, hurricanes, and earthquakes. Smaller would cover such illnesses as burns, blisters, and rashes.)

As the Hailway Chant was used to cure specific illnesses, or to avert major disasters, the Hailway Spread should be used to gain insight into a particular problem or concern troubling the seeker. A card to represent the querent should be selected and placed in the center of the table or floor. For guidelines to selecting this card, see page 147.

The motion of the Hailway Spread is upward and its number is seven. After the querent's card is placed, the diviner should shuffle the remaining deck and have the querent, while carefully pondering all aspects of the current problem, cut the deck seven times. The diviner should turn the cards over from left to right, and, as shown in the Hailway Spread diagram, begin at the base of the zigzag lightning and work upward in a zigzag pattern with the querent's card lying in the diagonal path between the numbers 'six' and 'seven' (see diagram).

The general pattern of the layout is determined in three portions: past, present, and future.

The Hailway Spread

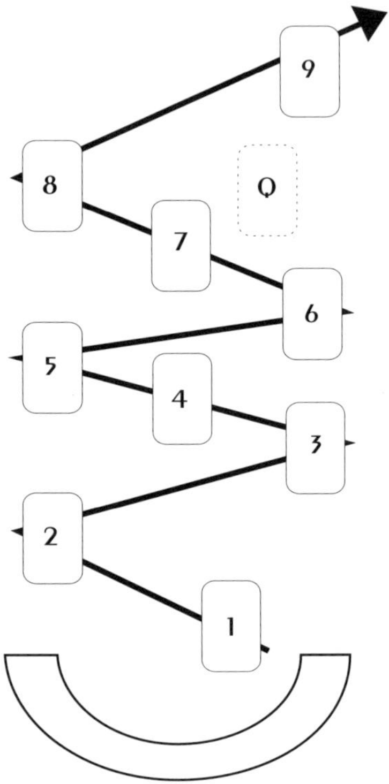

1. The Distant Past.
2. The Recent Past.
3. The Focal Point.
4. Immediate Influence.
5. External Influence.
6. Internal Influence.
7. Hopes and Fears.
8. Future Influence.
9. Culmination.

Q. The Questioner (also called Seeker or Querent.)

The significance of the cards in the Hailway Spread is as follows:

Card 1 The Distant Past. This card reflects the broad and basic events and influences which existed in the past and which contributed to the problem in question.

Card 2 The Recent Past. This card indicates, in context of the question, the most recent sphere of influence or events that has passed or is just passing.

Card 3 The Focal Point. This card reveals that combination of past and present events, and the influences resulting from them, that continue to affect the questioner at the current time.

Card 4 Immediate Influence. This card indicates the nature of the influences or the obstacles that surround the seeker at the present time.

Card 5 External Influence. This card shows the influences of those people within the seeker's close environment and how they might relate to the current question.

Card 6 Internal Influence. This card reflects the seeker's ability to effect change in the immediate present, how he or she relates to others, how the seeker might direct events.

Card 7 Hopes and Fears. This card expresses the seeker's innermost wishes or fears of the final resolution of the problem. A card showing a negative quality should be interpreted as revealing fears while a positive card reflects hopes.

Card 8 Future Influence. This card reveals, in a broad spectrum, the general influences or obstacles that will soon be coming to pass.

Card 9 Culmination. This card signifies the thrust upward of the lightning bolt, the breaking free of the problem at hand. A card that might ordinarily be regarded as negative might reveal, in this case, a course of action required, a necessary conflict or strife before positive resolution can occur.

(Note: As the seeker's representative card lies between the sixth and seventh position, which are the locations revealing the largest degree of the seeker's emotions, great care should be taken when discussing these feelings. Often the greatest problem to be resolved is that which lies within.)

Ancient Celtic Cross Method

Closely related to the modern 10-Card Spread, the Ancient Celtic Cross Method was first brought into accepted usage by Arthur Edward Waite in his book *The Pictorial Key to the Tarot*. The Celtic Cross Method has long been cited as one of the most popular and effective means of using the Tarot for divination.

The Celtic Cross Method is widely hailed as the diviner's diviner, showing that it can be used by the diviner, for the diviner, or can be used to aid a seeker, or, in its largest sense, the world itself.

Tradition calls for a card to represent the querent or seeker. In the case of the diviner or the seeker, one of the Court cards should be selected to indicate the querent. For information about selecting this card, see page 147.

If the diviner is reading for the world at large, the Major Arcana card, The World, should stand as representative. Occasionally, a diviner will wish to select an individual card from either the Major or Minor Arcana decks to seek specific insight into a particular matter. For a question relating to the purchase of a home, for example, the diviner might select the Ten of Buffalo card to represent the ideal, and upon reading the remaining cards, determine the obstacles and influences that could be brought to bear upon the purchase.

The cards should be shuffled by the diviner, and cut three times (to the left) by the seeker, unless the diviner wishes the vibrations of the seeker to saturate the cards, in which case the seeker should both shuffle and cut the cards. (The question of who shuffles the cards should be left to the discretion of the diviner.)

Following the pattern shown in the Celtic Cross diagram, place the first card over the seeker's card and the next card across it, and so on.

Ancient Celtic Cross Method

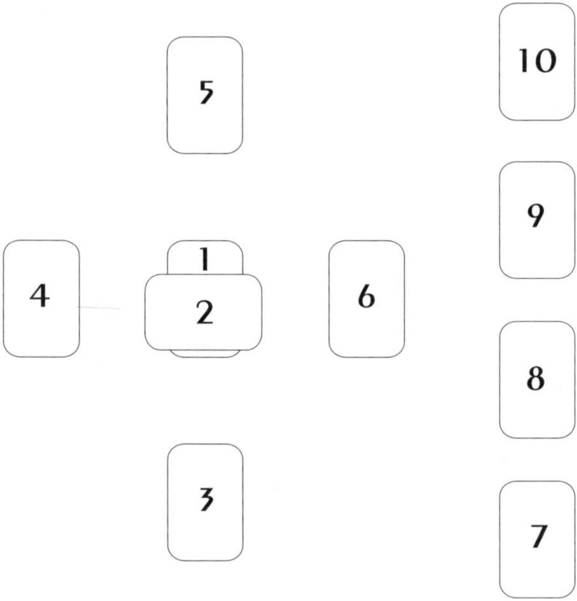

1. Covers The Seeker.
2. Crosses The Seeker.
3. Beneath The Seeker.
4. Behind The Seeker.
5. Crowns The Seeker.
6. Before The Seeker.
7. The Seeker's Fears.
8. Family Opinion.
9. Seeker's Hopes.
10. Final Outcome.

The significance of the cards in the 10-Card Spread is as follows:

Card 1 Covers the Seeker. This card reveals the general atmosphere surrounding the querent and the influences presently affecting the question.

Card 2 Crosses the Seeker. Laid across the cover card, this card reflects the nature of the influences or the obstacles that lie just ahead. This card is always read in upright position.

Card 3 Beneath the Seeker. This card reveals the basis of the matter at hand, something already part of the seeker's past.

Card 4 Behind the Seeker. This card reveals the recent past and the broad and basic events and influences upon which the present events are based.

Card 5 Crowns the Seeker. This card reveals something that may happen to the seeker (or the question) in the near future.

Card 6 Before the Seeker. This card reveals things that will happen in the immediate future. This may be reflected as an actual event or as an influence.

Card 7 The Seeker's Fears. This card reveals the negative feelings of seeker in relation to the question posed.

Card 8 Family Opinion. This card represents the seeker's environment, the opinions and influence of family and friends in relation to the question.

Card 9 Seeker's Hopes. This card represents the seeker's inner hopes and ideals about the question.

CARD 10 FINAL OUTCOME. This final card reveals the culmination of all that has been shown by the other cards. It should never be taken independently, but as a reflection of all the cards shown.

6

Glossary of Navajo Terms

Navajo language, unrecorded in written form until World War II, is largely transliterative; the spelling is reflective of the sound of the word when spoken. As the language consists of glottal stops, tonal changes, and gutturals, many of the spellings may vary from Navajo to Navajo.

The following Navajo names are those used within the confines of the Santa Fe Tarot book and, as with any language, represent a fraction of the total language.

AY-YAH-NEH: The Buffalo People

B'GANNASKIDDY: Humped-back Yei

DIN'NEH: The People

DO'TSOH: Fire Monsters

HA'ATATHLI: Medicine Man

HASH-JAISH-JINNH: The Black Gods

HASH-TYE-DIN'NEH: The Magic People

HOH'ZHO-OH-LI: The Blessingway

IKNE'ETSO: Big Thunder

NA'A-TSE-ELIT: The Rainbow People

NAHAS-TSAN-BEHASSUN: Mother Earth

NAYENEZGANI: Monster Slayer, Slayer-of-Alien-Gods

TE-O-SOL-HI: Water Monster

TOBASCHICHIN: Born of Water, Fighting Water, First Born

TRAHDAH-DE'EN-ESHKI: Pollen Boy

YAAH-DKLITH-BEH-HASTEEN: Father Sky

YEI: A god

YEI-BIH-CHAI: Another name for a god

YEI-TSO: A monster god

ZIA: A sun symbol

7

Suggested Reading List

Astrov, Margot. *American Indian Prose and Poetry, 'The Winged Serpent.'* New York, NY: Capricorn Books, 1962.

Bierhorst, John, ed. *In The Trail of the Wind, American Indian Poems and Ritual Orations.* New York, NY: Farrar, Straus and Giroux, 1971.

Bateman, Walter L. *The Navajo of the Painted Desert.* Boston, MA: Beacon Press, 1970.

Butler, Bill. *Dictionary of the Tarot.* New York, NY: Schocken Books, 1975.

Faris, James C. *The Nightway, A History and History of Documentation of a Navajo Ceremonial.* Albuquerque, NM: University of New Mexico Press, 1990.

Gray, Eden. *A Complete Guide to the Tarot.* New York, NY: Crown Publishers, 1970.

Gray, Eden. *Mastering the Tarot.* New York, NY: New American Library, 1971.

Kaplan, Stuart R. *The Encyclopedia of the Tarot, Volumes I, II & III.* Stamford, CT: U.S. Games Systems, Inc.

Keegan, Marcia. *Mother Earth, Father Sky—Navajo and Pueblo Indians of the Southwest*. New York, NY: Grossman Publishers, 1974.

Newcomb, Franc Johnson. *Navaho Folk Tales*. Museum of Navaho Ceremonial Art, 1967.

Newcomb, Franc Johnson. *Navajo Omens and Taboos*. Santa Fe, NM: Rydal Press, 1940.

Newcomb, Franc Johnson. *Hosteen Klah, Navaho Medicine Man and Sand Painter*. Norman, OK: University of Oklahoma Press, 1964.

Newcomb, Franc Johnson. *Navaho Neighbors*. Norman, OK: University of Oklahoma Press, 1966.

Villaseñor, David. *Tapestries in Sand, The Spirit of Indian Sandpainting*. Healdsburg, CA: Naturegraph Company, 1963, 1966.

Wall, Leon. N*avajo-English Dictionary*. Phoenix Indian School, AZ: Phoenix Press, 1958.

Wyman, Leland C. *The Windways of the Navaho*. The Taylor Museum of the Colorado Fine Arts Center, 1962.

Wyman, Leland C. *Blessingway*. Tucson, AZ: The University of Arizona Press, 1970.

8

About The Illustrator/Author

Lifetime residents of New Mexico, sisters Holly Huber and Tracy LeCocq have been long fascinated with the unique Navajo sandpaintings and their mystical qualities. After extensive research of Navajo symbology and mythology, the two women began exploring the possibilities of correlating Navajo myths with traditional Tarot. Both sisters believed it of vast importance to maintain the integrity of both ancient art forms and have done so in the unique design and composition of The Santa Fe Tarot Deck.

Their collaboration was not merely one of one drawing, the other writing; together they researched each story, myth, and chant, selecting individual components most suited to the Tarot while preserving the essential mystical elements of the sandpainting. The project, some five years in the making, marked a turning point in their own personal development and search for the Path of Beauty.

Holly Huber holds degrees in art, history, graphic design, communications, and education. A graphic design professor at Minot State University, in Minot, North Dakota, her expertise and distinctive style is recognizable in all her works.

Award-winning novelist Tracy LeCocq resides in Portales, New Mexico. She began her writing career as both a print and television journalist and now writes full-time, having penned more than ten Silhouette romantic-suspense novels under her pseudonym, Marilyn Tracy.

May my house be in harmony
From my head, may it be happy
To my feet, may it be happy
Where I lie, may it be happy
All above me, may it be happy
All around me, may it be happy.
Navajo